W9-AQB-746

Books by Morton Kelsey

Tongue Speaking

God, Dreams, and Revelation:
  A Christian Interpretation of Dreams

Encounter With God:
  A Theology of Christian Experience

Healing and Christianity

Myth, History and Faith:
  The Remythologizing of Christianity

The Christian and the Supernatural

The Other Side of Silence:
  A Guide to Christian Meditation

Can Christians Be Educated?:
  A Proposal for Effective Communication
  of Our Christian Religion

The Hinge:
  Meditations on the Cross

Discernment:
  A Study in Ecstasy and Evil

Dreams:
  A Way to Listen to God

Tales to Tell:
  Legends of the Senecas

The Age of Miracles:
  Seven Journeys to Faith

Afterlife:
  The Other Side of Dying

Adventure
INWARD

Adventure
INWARD

Christian Growth through Personal Journal Writing

Morton T. Kelsey

Augsburg Publishing House
Minneapolis, Minnesota

ADVENTURE INWARD

MANUFACTURED IN THE UNITED STATES OF AMERICA

To my youngest grandchild, Kenny Johnson—
that we may become as little children and enter the kingdom

Contents

Preface

For THIRTY YEARS my journal has been my constant companion. My daily writing in its pages has been a most helpful practice in my attempt to grow into the fullness of Christ. The journal has sustained me in darkness and given me a thread to find my way back into the light. It has provided a place where I could come to clarity and insight. It has recorded and stimulated my journey toward the loving God. It has opened the door for me to see the hand of the prodigal Father outreached to me, and allowed me to come to his forgiving embrace.

Great diaries have always been fascinating reading. They always contain reflection as well as naked data. Some of the greatest Christian devotional classics are simply the records men and women have made of their spiritual interaction with God.

Most people have thought that only gifted or important people would have anything of value to record in a journal. No one has done more to popularize journal keeping for ordinary men and women than Ira Progoff in his Intensive Journal Workshops. His book, *At a Journal Workshop,* describes the process which takes place at these events. It has been widely read.

In recent years there has been a renewed understanding of the value of keeping records of one's outer and inner life. Many books have been published on the practice of journal keeping. Many of them offer helpful suggestions. There is none, however, which presents the practice of journal keeping within the context and framework of the Christian life. Most of these books are secular or only incidentally religious. None of them points out the distinctive quality of a journal kept by a person who is trying to grow in relationship with the risen Christ.

The Christian view of the world provides a unique theory about journal keeping and a significantly different practice of doing it. Many people have found that secular instructions about journal keeping do not lead them toward their goal of Christian growth. Many people have asked me to speak about journal keeping at conferences. The director of book development for Augsburg Publishing House has encouraged me to write down what I have learned about Christian journal keeping in 30 years of practicing it. In the pages which follow I have tried to be practical and specific, giving a step-by-step method by which one can use a journal as a means of aiding and stimulating growth in one's Christian life.

This book is written as a guide for one who wishes to keep a religious journal. If one simply reads through the book at one or two sittings and does not start a journal, the book has failed in its purpose. I would suggest using the book in the following way. First, read it through quickly to grasp the basic idea of journal keeping. If you then decide that journal keeping within this context is for you, start again and move from chapter to chapter, keeping a journal as you go along. Use what is presented as a launching pad for your own practice.

The first suggestions for journal keeping are quite direct and simple. I then lead readers deeper and deeper into the human psyche on a spiral staircase. I look at some of the same issues and problems several times, but each time from a deeper and different perspective. To casual readers this process may appear repetitious. There is, however, a progression which one will recognize as one works in depth with a journal. It is also important to remember that journal keeping is a living process, like exercise. One does the same thing over and over to develop and maintain a skill. Healthy living in body and soul and mind requires the constant repetition of certain practices. A book on journal writing will of necessity emphasize the same thing more than once.

This book can be read by itself. However, what is written here will be better understood if it is read along with my book *The Other Side of Silence* (Paulist, 1976). That book on Christian imagination and meditation provides a theory of the development of the inner Christian life. This present book offers a method by which the theory of that book can be put into practice.

I am deeply grateful to my wife, Barbara, who has read over every word of this manuscript many times and who has even listened to me read it to her. In some ways this book is as much hers as mine. It could never have been written without her sustaining help, which has freed me to write, and her encouragement to get these ideas down in a style which can reach ordinary Christian readers. I am also grateful to Rosalind Winkelholz and her daughter Leslie for retyping and correcting my inimitable typing and putting it into legible form.

MORTON T. KELSEY
Gualala, California
Pentecost 1979

1

Why Keep
a Journal?

P EOPLE HAVE BEEN keeping records of their lives for a
long time. As soon as human beings learned to write they
began to record their thoughts and deeds and hopes. Sometimes these records have come down to us by accident. The
almost indestructible Near Eastern cuneiform writings on
clay tablets dug up thousands of years later tell us of business transactions, personal interchanges between lovers, and
mythical and religious stories. The scribblings on potsherds
from ancient Greece give the same kind of picture of life
in that region. Papyrus documents which survived in the
dry sands of Egypt give us glimpses of life in the valley
of the Nile.

Quite different are the records which scribes have left of
great conquerors, kings, important officials, and significant
events. Sometimes these records are part history and part
mythology. Sometimes tales of myth and religion stand
alone. Some records are found carved into rock in tombs or
in triumphal arches, written in the most imperishable mate-
rials available. In most settled cultures there are libraries of
these records. One of the great tragedies of warfare and

conquest is that these records are often destroyed and lost. In China, where society has continued for 3500 years without total interruption or collapse, these records are continuous and intact for that entire period.

The desire to record and reflect upon one's life seems to be an almost instinctual human need. Whenever humans have risen out of a tribal identity and have come to see themselves as separate from other human beings and having individual value, they want to leave some record for their children, for the world, for fate. Although ordinary men and women cannot erect a Taj Mahal or an Egyptian tomb depicting their deeds, they can leave behind a tombstone, and most do.

In the last several hundred years three great changes have taken place in the quality of human life. These changes started in Western Europe and have spread all over the world. These new developments have made it possible for ordinary human beings to make records of their outer and inner lives. The keeping of a journal has been brought within the grasp of nearly every man and woman.

First of all there has been an increasing emphasis on education for ordinary people. Widespread literacy is scarcely a century old. Seldom do we realize how recent is the movement toward universal education which enables average persons to read and write. There are many areas in the world where ordinary people still do not have these tools for conscious and reflective living. Several centuries ago even lords and conquerors, the wealthy and the powerful, could not read or write themselves. They had to hire scribes to record their letters and thoughts. Only persons who can write are going to put down all that comes to mind as they stop and turn inward.

Second, men and women must believe that their lives are

important and have value if they are going to go to the trouble of recording them. During this same period of time there has been a growing awareness that ordinary people have as much value as the educated and powerful. Only in the last century have novels or operas or dramas been written about peasants, tradespeople, and townspeople. The value of ordinary people is a uniquely Western idea springing from our Judeo-Christian heritage. It doesn't make much sense to record the concrete events of one's life if they are *maya* or illusion. And this is the point of view of most Eastern religions and most Eastern people. In the West the new attitude toward common people has also clearly contributed to the movement toward general education.

Third, it is only within recent years that cheap tools for writing have been easily available. Sheepskin, parchment, and papyrus were expensive commodities.

Thus it is only within the last hundred years or so that conditions have been right for general journal keeping. What had been the practice of poets and writers, scribes and the educated few is now available to most human beings in the Western world and many people elsewhere. As we turn inward and begin to make a record of ourselves we find that new vistas open up and new potentials for growth appear. Depth and creativity within us emerge which we never dreamed were there. Many of us have far more to write about than we thought. As we dig wells into our own inner beings through keeping some kind of record of these selves, we find that there is living water within each of us. We can tap into it directly. We do not need to rely solely on others for the water of life.

Because the possibilities for this kind of practice are so recent, there are few simple, practical, or generally accepted directions about why an ordinary person may want to keep a journal or how one goes about using an inner log in order to get the most out of it. In recent years there have been a number of books on the subject. Most of these are secular or at least do not integrate an individual's religious practice. It is my purpose to look at the journal as a part of the total religious process—the journal as one very important and perhaps essential aspect of the growing person's religious life.

A book of many uses

There are many, many reasons for keeping a journal, and a whole book could easily be written on each of them. The most common and most consistent use of such writing throughout history is the simple need to keep records. We fallible humans do not always remember what we need to remember. Whether for business or pleasure, we need to keep a record. Some years ago, my wife and I had the trip of our lives. We spent seven months traveling around Southeast Asia, Australia, and New Zealand. We came home through the Pacific Islands, Thailand, India, Turkey, the Holy Land, and Europe. A friend gave me a journal setup to keep a record of our trip. As I look back through this diary the joy of that trip comes back to life and I can relive it. Ordinarily my life does not have that kind of variety, but I still need some record of it if I am not to lose many parts of it. How often it is that I cannot remember what happened last Tuesday, let alone last year on this day! A journal gives some sense of continuity and depth to our lives.

History is the record of what men and women have thought and done. When we keep a record of our lives we step into the fabric of history and record our part in that process. Often the diaries of obscure people give us a picture of life in another time and age which more official histories leave untouched. How much richer we are for having both kinds of records! An unknown scribe living at the time of King David wrote the magnificent story of the great king recorded in the Second Book of Samuel. Xenophon recorded the retreat of his mercenary soldiers in the service of Cyrus. Caesar wrote of his conquest of Gaul.

Whenever we have participated in some great event there is a strong urge to keep it vividly before us. If we were invited to Buckingham Palace or the White House it would be quite natural to sit down and write out what we saw and experienced. Few of us have such opportunities, but each of us has the opportunity to relate to one far greater. Christians believe that God, the divine lover, seeks our friendship and companionship. We can experience this encounter in outer events or rituals, through human contacts, or through our inward turning. When we do not make some record of our experiences of God, it is almost as if we devalue them.

In the Gospels we have the records of those who had experienced God in a particular human being, Jesus of Nazareth, and found that this experience continued after Jesus was no longer physically with them. How much poorer all of us would be if they had not recorded their experiences! Keeping a journal puts us in a position to record both outer events and inner ones. We can use this record at a later time for our own reflection or to share with others.

A second reason for keeping a journal is simply because it is fun to record what we are thinking and feeling. For some people it is play to sit down and let the words flow out in stories and images. For those who have not been spoiled by a faulty and bungling educational system, writing can be a form of play. Some like to dance when the mood takes them, some pick up crayons or paintbrushes and draw, some go out in the garden and dig and plant, and some try to cook a particularly creative meal. Others like to play with words. They let words tumble over each other and take whatever forms they seem to want to have. For these people, writing in a journal can be a creative expression of their inner lives.

Unfortunately, few schools teach children to enjoy using words in this way. In most schools, writing is deadly serious business which must include proper grammar and spelling, neat and legible handwriting, and proper margins. Nothing kills the creative use of writing more than this kind of teaching. If we are going to use a journal freely and happily, we need first of all to cease seeing it as an onerous exercise. Just as religious ritual loses its power and majesty when it becomes an obligation, so writing a journal goes sour when it is something that must be done as exercises in a copybook. A journal properly used is like a playground into which we can step and play when we are alone.

It is only a short step from using a journal as a place in which one can play to using one's notebook as the raw material for the creative artistic drive. It is hard to describe the nature of art. In my opinion, we have art whenever the eternal is expressed in concrete form. It is archetypal reality shining through our creation. Great art is simply that which touches a universal aspect of spiritual reality in such form that it touches the lives of many people.

Few people have paints and brushes, drawing books, or canvases available. Few have enough skill to give satisfaction in painting or weaving or gardening, but all literate people can write and can have a notebook available. We have everything we need to begin the artistry of words. Most of us can write poetry, tell stories, or record interesting narratives. There is more of the poet in us than we realize. It is nearly impossible to get far in allowing this side of ourselves expression until we begin to record the emotions and attitudes and images which begin to stir within us when we are quiet and turn inward.

Most of us are far more creative than we have been led to believe. A journal can also be used as a method of allowing our inner creativity to be released. By recording who and what we are, our feelings, our hopes and goals, we break the hard crust of our selves and allow the depth of us to bubble up into sight. So much of our lives is spent in going the daily round and doing the expected thing in business, family life, and recreation that we do not get in touch with the deeper levels of ourselves. We do not even know our deep inner springs of creativity. I wonder if it is possible for average men and women truly to believe the depth of their creative beings unless they have taken time and written down some of their creative sparks of thought and insight and then looked back on them at a later time. Some people use a journal mainly as a way of getting in touch with their individual creativity. This creativity can take many forms. In addition to thoughts and philosophical musings, the creative urge may be expressed in descriptions of a vivid scene, a powerful encounter with another person, or insights which come almost out of the blue.

There is a close connection between creativity and imagination. Still another use of a journal is to help us release our imagination. As we release our imagination we begin to touch our creative inner depths and the poet hidden in each of us. Imagination is something which can be learned and taught. Some people are greatly gifted with native imagination. Others have little, but many can develop this capacity. They can learn to think in images which bring them in touch with a whole aspect of reality which sense experience and reason do not often reveal. A journal can aid one in encouraging the imagination and allowing it to grow within us. For some people the only value of an inner log is to stimulate imagination, creativity, and artistic creation. Many writers have published their journals. The very recording of their inner and outer lives can be an imaginative, creative art form. The journals of Anais Nin are a good example. We shall have more to say about how to use a journal to stimulate imagination. Jung has pointed out that some people use their imagination only artistically. They often fail to realize that it can bring them in touch with another dimension of reality which needs serious attention.

Images and emotions are closely interrelated. A person adept at yoga learns to control emotions. One of the methods of gaining control over them is to erase all images from before one's mind. Eastern and Western thought value images and emotions very differently. Emotions are those human experiences in which inner attitudes are combined with a physiological response on the part of the body. In the East emotions are seen as tying one into dependence on the outer physical world, on *maya*. In the West emotions can be seen as valuable because they relate one to the real physical world. Emotions of fear, anxiety, and hatred can tie one into that world in a destructive way. When the emotion of love is pursued it can lead to the very core and center of reality, to the divine lover.

In a journal one can pour out whatever emotions arise within one without fear of embarrassment or of hurting or putting another person on the spot. Emotions are evanescent and fragile (and at the same time powerful). It is difficult to know the powers and drives and feelings which move and direct us unless we look at these emotions and record them. Often we do not know how angry we are until we start writing a letter to someone who has betrayed us. We do not know how much we love until we let our feelings and emotions spill out on paper. It is almost impossible to deal with all of ourselves in a creative or objective way if we make no record of these emotional stirrings within us. Without a journal frequently used we remain out of touch with a large part of ourselves.

The many uses of a journal overlap one another. The expression of emotion, given form, can be poetry or art. Indeed there is little real artistic creativity which does not embody some deep outpouring of emotion. If one does not have the habit of recording the ebb and flow of one's inner life, one can be cut off from the whole playful, imaginative, creative aspect of life.

Reflection, healing, and growth

In *Homo Ludens* (Beacon, 1955) Johan Huizinga suggests that the ability to play may be more centrally characteristic of our humanness than our capacity to think. It is certainly true that whole human beings need to know how to play *and* think. A journal can be for some a serious tool for dealing with life as well as an instrument of play. Keeping a journal can be of inestimable value in helping one sort through the difficulties, problems, and possibilities of life in order to manage one's life as well as possible.

Few of us can hold together all the different threads of

our lives unless we put them down one by one. It is strange how we can forget very important parts of our lives until we sit before a blank piece of paper and put them down one by one. In order to gain objectivity before any important decision or many minor ones, it is valuable to take time to reflect. The habit of keeping a regular record of one's inner life prepares one for times of sorting, objectively looking at the data, and weighing the inner or outer situation. One friend often suggested the practice of a plus and minus chart to people faced with decisions, and this will be discussed in a later chapter.

A journal can help us make decisions and give us some objectivity. We could avoid many sad mistakes and much pain if we would learn to stop, reflect, write, and assess. This practice can be used in personal decisions, in business decisions, and in any situation where we need to weigh the evidence before we act. A journal used in this way gives us power over our own impulsiveness and enables us to take hold of life and run it with direction and purpose. Few of us like to be pawns of fate. Written reflection can begin to free us from the unconsciousness in which we live so much of the time.

Most people are suffering far more than others realize. Most of us put on our masks of self-reliance and jovial well-being when we go out to face the world. Most of us bear heavy burdens much of the time. Those who open themselves to listen in depth to others hear a great deal of inner turmoil and confusion. For many people survival is victory, and a journal is a helpful tool for survival. Although I had begun to keep a record of my life and my dreams earlier, I did not truly learn to understand the potential value of a journal until I used one to help me out of the pit. One of the most important things I learned from my friend Max Zeller was how to use a journal for survival.

Writing down emotions in poetic form is one matter. Describing emotions of fear and anger, hopelessness and depression, compulsivity and stress is quite another. Giving expression in the written word to the feelings which appear about to overwhelm and possess us often gives us distance from them. Then we begin to take control over our own lives. When we live on top of an emotional volcano which is about to erupt, recording our feelings can help us move off it or even keep the explosion from occurring.

As a healing or therapeutic tool a journal is invaluable. It gives a space to deal with the cause of inner turmoil. We can bring many problems and fears into the open and deal with them face to face in honest combat. In a journal we can distinguish between friends and foes. This kind of reflection can transform a street fight into a more or less orderly athletic event. In the pages of a journal we can deal with concerns about our body, marriage, sexuality, fear of death, immortality, or anything else. We can also turn and talk to any inner part of ourselves. We can speak with the inner child or inner adolescent or any other part of us which has been left behind as we grew to physical and professional maturity. A journal is an ever-present friend with whom we can discuss anything.

Many over-the-counter medicine bottles warn that a physician should be consulted if the symptoms do not disappear in a certain number of days. The same advice should be printed on all journals. When pain or agony, confusion and depression continue, we should seek someone who has been through the dark waters and found a way through. The very keeping of a journal may clarify the situation to such a point that we realize that we need help with this inner confusion.

One of the most interesting accounts of the therapeutic use of a journal is the book by Duane Mehl, *No More for the Road* (Augsburg, 1976). With utter honesty the author describes how he used a journal in connection with the 12 steps of Alcoholics Anonymous. He brought himself from utter defeat to effective living. He shows how helpful a journal is in enabling one to honestly reflect on one's life. Only with such a base can a life be turned around and changed.

Some people may turn to a journal just because they want to grow and develop or come to know themselves better. My opinion, however, is that few people get interested in their growth and development, in their self-knowledge and self-education, unless they have experienced some inner pain. The seed seldom grows until something has cracked the husk of its potentiality and allowed its life to germinate and begin to grow. When one's husk is being cracked open one is seldom sure whether this is just a painful and necessary process or whether it is indeed the very destruction of one's being. If human children were endowed with full consciousness at birth, they would describe a harrowing experience which at times, in the midst of the process, must have looked like a dead-end street. Stanislav Grof has pointed out in two of his books that the rebirth experience discovered in LSD therapy presents the same terror and struggle.

Once a seed has begun to grow into a plant or tree it has to continue to grow or else it will die. The same is true of a human being who starts on the inner journey. It is important to stress at this point that *this inner journey is not for everyone*. Nearly everyone can profit by keeping a record of one's inner life and how one is doing in the world, but this striving for growth and development and self-knowledge for its own sake is not the way all of us should go. Unfortunately, not all the advocates of journaling for growth stress the dangers involved or the selective nature of this kind of process. Some plants can survive in nearly any environment, while others require tender care or even a hothouse.

And then there are those who use journals as tools for curious exploration of the hidden depths of reality. Some people become fascinated by the richness and depth of spiritual reality. They explore it for curiosity, not realizing the dangers involved. Playing around with these depths (often called the occult) is dangerous. Without proper care one can get lost within the inner world and even come to mental illness. Of this we shall say more later.

If it is inner growth and self-knowledge which is one's goal, for whatever reason, this process is nearly impossible without journal keeping. There is a creative urge within most individuals toward inner growth and greater understanding, better integration of one's life, deeper use of one's creativity, toward developing to the maximum of one's potential. There is no better book on this aspect of journal keeping than Ira Progoff's *At a Journal Workshop* (Dialogue House, 1975). He believes there is an inner depth of creative, healthy life within humans which can be tapped by the use of a journal, leading one almost inevitably toward the goal of wholeness and maturity. Dr. Progoff, however, does not describe very clearly what this ultimate state of human beings is like or how one can tell whether one is approaching this ideal or not.

In *Keeping Your Personal Journal* (Paulist, 1978) George Simons stresses the value of keeping a journal as part of the educational process within a classroom setting. As one records one's situation at the beginning of a course of study and then goes on to record new insights and understandings, one can chart one's progress. Such a journal can even point out areas where further study and work are needed and help one's educational journey. It is but a short step from this use of a journal to using a journal as a means of self-help and self-growth. When the subject of one's study becomes one's self, then a journal becomes a means for digging into one's self and finding what forces are operating within. Then the effort will be to bring this whole person to the highest possible stage of development and growth.

A journal as a way of relating to God

There is yet another and quite different reason for keeping a journal. The goal here is not simply that of achieving my own potential, but rather of deepening my relationship with that center of spiritual reality of which all the great religions of humankind speak. Here the goal of keeping the record of my life and struggle is not so much to forge the chain of growth as to bring my inner being to the blacksmith. The journal is not so much an integral part of the building as a scaffolding which is needed to construct the building and then needed later to repair the structure.

But the size of the building one can construct without scaffolding is limited indeed. The deep relationship with God which can be received and integrated in many men and women is limited by the amount of effort and time and discipline they will take to keep some record of their encounters with religious reality. Journals record these encounters and are also useful tools for keeping at the process of developing the relationship. They can also point out new ways to open one's being to God's transforming power. I doubt whether those who can read and write are able to come to the deep relationship with the divine lover which is possible for them if they do not keep a journal.

Keeping a journal can be beneficial for all of the foregoing reasons, but will not thereby necessarily lead to a relationship with God. We can keep a record of the world around us and of our participation in its events, and this can be helpful in understanding ourselves and may offer important lessons for those who follow after us. Such journal keeping, however, can lead to self-aggrandizement and egotism as often as bringing us to the religious center of reality.

One can keep an exciting and delightfully written record of one's inner life, and it can still end in a dead-end street religiously. It may be playful, charming, full of fun, and yet come in the end to despair and disillusionment. If one knows how to follow playfulness and humor to God, one can find the way; but this road does not inevitably lead there. The great existential writers like Camus and Sartre lead usually to despair.

It is good to use a journal as a log of one's inner thoughts and experiences. This can help us in managing our lives and bringing healing to many of our hurts. Yet we can be healed of a specific illness and still not find wholeness. A therapist friend of mine complains that many people get just enough help so they no longer are hurting rather than pursuing the inner journey to the divine center of reality, which brings inner meaning. One can use a journal to ameliorate one's inner pain and confusion and still not find one's way to God himself. One must be very sensitive indeed to one's inner being to allow pain to lead one to a relationship with God.

A journal is certainly one of the most important tools on the journey of self-discovery and self-actualization. This is not, however, necessarily the greatest, finest, or final goal of life. If indeed there is a loving reality at the heart of the universe, finding this transforming reality is as important a goal as working at one's own growth and development. Being found by God is the purpose of most great religions. This discovery requires special knowledge, or even revelation. The path of self-growth does not necessarily lead toward this goal.

If, indeed, there is a Spirit of love which is the central organizing force in the cosmos, then coming to know and relate to this reality with all of our being is the final end of living and the final goal of existence. The other uses of journals are valuable by themselves, but they do not necessarily lead to a relationship with God.

However, if I pursue the path of a relationship with God, then sooner or later I will use a journal for each of these other reasons as well. If I am to come to God, to truly come to him, then I must bring all of myself to this one who seeks me out. One cannot develop and grow in this relationship without learning to use many of the skills and techniques that have been suggested for keeping the most complete record of one's life. God is interested in all parts of us. He is interested in our outer lives and our effectiveness in them. He is also concerned with the effect we have on others. Being the source of humor and play, he wants us to learn to play and enjoy his creation, and even more to enjoy him. Within the Christian tradition healing of the sick and confused was one of the most significant ministries of Jesus of Nazareth, who was the very Spirit of love incarnate. God cares about our hurt and pain. And since God has placed a potential for growth within us, he is concerned that we grow into the fullness of the sons and daughters of God.

It is not a matter of *either* using a journal to seek a relationship with God *or* using a journal to help us grow in our effectiveness in both the outer and inner worlds. We begin to realize our potential when we use a journal for *both* purposes. The question we need to ask ourselves is, What is my central purpose for keeping a journal? If my goal is to bring all of myself to God for redemption, renewal, and transformation, I will need to use all the practices which I have described. But if my primary reason for using a journal is only personal growth, I can quite easily avoid the goal of a relationship with God.

There are many books about journal writing. There is none that I know of which treats journal keeping as one part of the process of coming to a transforming encounter with God. How I keep a journal will depend on my central goal in keeping such a record and thus will determine the amount of time I spend in the various journal activities I have described. I will be giving suggestions and practices, guidelines and exercises in journal writing from the perspective of the person whose main goal is to be found and transformed by God, the divine lover, revealed in Jesus Christ. Depth psychology can offer modern men and women help in achieving this goal.

God made human beings to have great depth and complexity. It is one thing to come to an intellectual acceptance of Christianity. It is another to bring the whole of one's self to God for leavening of the entire person. I shall be offering methods by which a journal can be used for this latter process.

2

What Kind
of Journal?

T HE FIRST STEP in keeping a journal is to buy a journal book and have it available. Scraps or odd sheets of paper will not do. The way we keep our inner jottings is often a sign and symbol of how we value them. A journal is the symbol of one's inner life, and from my point of view it is a sign of how important we consider our encounter with God to be. If I can really relate to the one who cares for me more than I ever imagined and yet do not keep some record of that relationship, I may be showing how unimportant that relationship really is to me. If I keep the record on scraps of paper which are lost and scattered, I may again be indicating either that I don't think God is real or else in writing I was only trying to follow a will-o'-the-wisp or a wishful fantasy.

Anyone who has been in love knows what letters and cards from one's beloved mean. They are sacraments of that love, almost holy to us. We usually keep them in a special place. Often when someone has died and we go through their possessions, we will find such letters carefully put away. This is as true of men as of women.

As we grow in our relationship to God, we find that his love is different, greater, and more consistent than that of any human being. It is true that human love can open us to the vision of what divine love is. But human love is flawed by quarrels, misunderstandings, and hurt feelings, and then there is always death which separates us. As we learn to use a journal it can become a record of the incredible love God has for us. A journal can become a packet of love letters from God, letters which speak to us in our special need and try to draw us forth into the fruition of our potential in the presence of the loving God. A record or a notebook such as this is truly holy.

There are two reasons for having a permanent copybook which is set aside for the purpose of one's inner journey. First of all it is, as we have indicated, a sacred record. But almost as important as that, it stimulates us to keep up the relationship. When one is truly in love, nothing is worse than not getting a letter from the one who cares about us and for whom we care. A journal keeps the letters flowing. One cannot do much in learning to play a piano without having one available. An imitation keyboard is satisfactory for only so long. It is sometimes difficult to afford a piano or find a place to keep it. But anyone can afford a journal and find a place to house it.

The mechanics of a journal

Sometimes we do not start valuable practices simply because we do not know how to begin. Some people have been to a Progoff Intensive Journal Workshop or read his book on these workshops. From that point of view keeping a journal is a very complicated and involved process which

may seem overwhelming. If one doesn't follow his suggestions, what does one do?

Caught in this kind of indecision and questioning, one
often does nothing. I am reminded of the delightful story
of the laborer who had no work and came to a farmer for
something to do. The farmer sent him into his potato barn
to sort potatoes in three sizes: large, medium, and small.
When the farmer came home at the end of the day, the hired
man was found sitting in front of the potatoes, looking very
frustrated. None had been sorted. When he was asked what
the trouble was, he answered in a pathetic tone: "Decisions,
decisions, decisions."

To start a journal requires making a decision. Find a notebook somewhere in the house, or go out and buy one. This
kind of action can be a truly religious one. When I first
decided to keep a journal, I found a book I had used in
seminary to copy down Hebrew words. There were many
unused pages in this bound, blank book of 300 pages. I continued to use such a journal until I began to travel and found
it to be too heavy to carry with me. However, it did have
the value of giving substantial form to my inner jottings.
I now find that a simple spiral or bound composition book
is just as adequate and costs much less.

Some may prefer an unlined black book, especially if they
like to add drawings or illuminated letters. The important
thing is to find a book with which you are comfortable and
with which you are happy. If you keep a journal for a long
time you may try dozens of different kinds of record books.
The important thing is to make a decision, acquire one, and
get started. The actual notebook should be large enough to
keep the record of a considerable period of time, but not so
large that it is difficult to carry. Little notebooks of 2 by 3

inches may not give enough space for one's inner reactions; however, it is possible to carry this size in one's pocket or purse and thus always have it along.

I keep a mechanical pencil clipped inside the book. It is seldom used for anything else. I like a thin pencil so that the composition book with the pencil is not too bulky. My wife prefers a fine-point pen; these make writing neater, as they never smudge.

On the cover I write my name, address, and phone number, and a note that if the book is lost I will pay a reward for its return. One value of the Progoff Intensive Journal is that each one has a number and is registered at the Progoff headquarters in New York. This preserves the anonymity of the book. If one has recorded in depth one's feelings and attitudes, reactions to other people, and most personal fantasies, one will not want this to fall into anyone's hands. What can be done to preserve the confidentiality of a journal?

A person living alone has fewer problems of confidentiality than one living with other people, married or in community. Whether one lives alone or with others, it is best not to leave a record of one's innermost feelings lying around. One might not mind having the more abstract conversations with God read, but expressions of anger, depression, and other feelings are not for the eyes of others. One reason for keeping a journal and talking and listening to the divine lover is the concern that no one else can understand or accept the totality of one's sexual fantasies, hurt feelings, or disappointments.

A journal left lying around may tempt the curiosity of the most virtuous. A journal in a drawer or locked in a file (or in a suitcase when one is traveling) tempts no one. Although I have discovered that few people are interested in my inner thoughts, if I think that what I am writing about might upset another person or be used against me, I can always use shorthand or code for certain key words, actions, or thoughts. Or I can change names around so that only I can understand the one to whom I am referring. A few such changes make a journal practically unintelligible to an outsider, but perfectly clear to the writer. It also spoils the journal for anyone who would use it against the writer legally. In addition, my handwriting is so abominable that only a handwriting expert could make much of it.

There are special situations in which one should be careful with a journal. When living with a spouse, child, or visitor who, one knows, is not motivated by similar values about the confidentiality of personal writing, one ought to keep the journal out of the way or hidden. This is particularly true when one's actions or thoughts might concern that other person. If one discusses matters which concern that other person and leaves the record around, one is asking for trouble. They *must be coded,* written in another notebook kept for such disclosures, or typed and kept in some secret file. Leaving a record that is embarrassing out in the open may be an unconscious wish to reveal that material, or may reflect an unconscious hostility which comes out by leaving the incriminating evidence where another person is tempted to read it.

Seldom is a relationship furthered by an unconscious revealing of inner angers, unfaithful actions, or evil intent. One purpose for keeping a journal is to grow in consciousness. If one is naive about leaving a journal around one can be falling into the unconscious. Naiveté has little place in recording one's inner life, except when it is indulged in with purpose. A young man with whom I was counseling left an incriminating letter from his girlfriend in his jeans when his mother washed them. Naturally she read it. This was the worst way of bringing up the subject of their relationship, and the young man was very much at a disadvantage when the subject was brought up.

Some people have a greater sense of privacy than others. Such persons will take even greater care in keeping the content of their journals from others. And what happens to our journals when we die? There are some things about us that we may not want to share with our children, our heirs, or our posterity. Recently when my wife faced surgery she burned a whole series of journals in which she had worked out certain problems. One can dispose of one's journals in one's will and one may direct that they be destroyed. A friend who teaches meditative prayer and journal keeping passed on this request. One can even have a sense of humor about such matters:

> Now I lay me down to sleep.
> I pray the Lord my soul to keep.
> If I should die before I wake,
> Throw my journal in the lake.

How to begin

Many of Ira Progoff's suggestions for work in a journal are very helpful, but I do not find that one's journal needs to be structured around them. I divide my journal into two basic parts. I write from the back forward as I record my dealings with myself, my emotions, my dealings with God and the unconscious. I work from the front of the journal for my more conscious thoughts, records, plans, and business jottings.

Once I have a notebook and a pencil in hand, how exactly do I begin?

1. First of all I date every entry and number every page in my copybook if it is not already numbered. The numbering enables me to find entries that I have written when I am looking for some item in the past. The dating helps in the same way and does a great deal more. It places me in a specific time and place, for along with the date I record where I am writing from if I am not at home. This grounds me into the concrete present and keeps me from wandering off into pure unconsciousness and becoming vague and too ethereal. The dating also reminds me each time I pick up the journal when I last wrote in it. It is truly astounding how we can avoid a practice which we have resolved to keep up. How difficult it is to carry on something as simple as a daily record of one's inner and outer life! When I pick up my journal and discover that I have not written in it for a week or several weeks, the dating is a strong reminder.

2. If one is keeping a journal for inner growth or as a record of one's inner and outer life, or as a help in dealing with pain, it may not be necessary to keep the journal daily. If, however, one is keeping this inner record as a way of stimulating and deepening one's relationship with God or as a record of that relationship with God, it is crucial to keep a daily record, a daily journal. If God is truly the divine lover, then a day lived without relationship or record of that relationship is a day which is less than full and whole.

It is also interesting to note that the very word *journal* indicates a daily practice. It comes from the Middle English word *journal* which was a daily service book containing the services to be said at different times during the day. This word came from the French word meaning "daily" and that from the Latin *diurnalis,* meaning "daily."

3. When I begin writing in a new journal, I write a page or so reviewing what has occurred in my inner and outer life during the course of the last journal and summarize this period of from six months to a year. I find that a daily journal lasts about that length of time. In beginning a journal for the first time, a good plan is to start by examining why you are beginning this practice, and where you are in your outer relationships, your relationship with yourself, and with God. If, however, this seems like a task that will keep you from starting, just begin with a date and start with one of the following entries.

A dream. I will say more about the recording of dreams later on, but at this point it is only necessary to point out that the recording of your dream can show what is going on within your unconscious life. Many people and cultures view dreams as God speaking within the soul. Dreams add another dimension to your journal and your reflections and push you quickly out of an ordinary, pedestrian way of thinking about yourself. A simple summary of a dream is all that is needed. If one is not brief, one can go on describing even a simple dream forever.

Reflections about the preceding day and some account of it. This is the beginning of a daily inner and outer log. It is not necessary to report everything. Indeed, making a simple summary stimulates you toward evaluating your life. As with a dream, one can describe everything and go on forever. For example, one can describe driving to the store for a loaf of bread, those whom one met in the store, and the sad fact that the bread that one desired was not there, as well as the decisions which this entailed. To get a perspective, write down in three sentences the important and valuable events and happenings of the day. Sometimes we don't even realize what we value until we begin such a practice. This kind of record begins to show us where our values are and what our priorities are. Through such a practice we begin to achieve some consciousness of who we are and what we are about, as well as an objective record for reflection and review.

There will be significant days when we will wish to write more. They may be full and meaningful or days in which we have experienced some new understanding about our friends or a new and vivid experience of God. When a day has been particularly meaningful, we should set aside a special time for recording and understanding it. But if we record only striking and exciting days, we find that we are likely to forget to record the ordinary days. We can learn nearly as much from our reflections on run-of-the-mill days as from the extraordinary ones. Daily recording requires commitment and perseverance.

Listening to the inner depth, to the inner guide, to God. I find I start a day awry when I do not bring the summary of my life and inner thoughts and dreams before the one who wishes to relate to me. As I pause and listen, something other than my ordinary typical, habitual attitudes speaks within me. It is hard to believe that there is another level of one's being which can speak. I know of no better way of testing the reality of this voice than setting aside time for this listening and recording. Some people find that nothing occurs to them when they are sitting with a journal and pencil in hand. They must do their listening, concentrating on this alone. However, if they do it, it is helpful to have a time for recording the insights and encounters which come during the time of listening.

4. Often when I begin to get still I find that I remember all sorts of things which I ought to have done, people I should have called, letters I should have written, clothes that should have been picked up at the cleaners, or bills that should have been paid. In a special little box I put these matters to be taken care of. If I try simply to remember them, I cannot get far in reflection or listening beyond myself.

5. Unless I have a time set aside for this kind of journal keeping, I will not keep a journal regularly. We live very different kinds of lives with very different rhythms. Each person needs to find the best time for daily reflection. I started by keeping a record of my dreams. I learned to get up in the middle of the night when I awoke. At that time practically no one ever bothered me and I was clear and open. For some people this time would be lethal.

It makes no difference when the time is. It may be the first thing in the morning, and may mean getting up 30 minutes earlier in the morning. It can be in the evening before retiring, keeping one up later at night. One may need time away from home and may stop at an open church on the way home from work. A busy homemaker may find that the best time is after everyone has left home. A mother with young children may find that their nap time is her only possible retreat into herself. Without finding a regular time that fits one's schedule, there will be no consistent journal keeping. Keeping a journal anytime one feels like it usually means keeping no journal at all. And a life which is not recorded and reflected upon is often a life only half lived.

There are other kinds of times which one needs if a journal is to be more than a daily log, but we shall speak of these at a later point.

6. At the opposite end of the notebook from the one in which I keep this daily dated log I keep many different things. Each person will find different uses for this part of their journal, depending on their profession and interests. Here are some of the things which I keep at this end of my journal:

A list of people for whom I pray. Those I love are mixed in with those who have offended me and those I find difficult to love. If the journal falls into the hands of an outsider they will be none the wiser, as my sheep cannot be separated from my goats.

Outlines for articles, sermons, and books. This is the conscious part of my journal. Here I list my ideas and try to organize them.

Important addresses and telephone numbers. There are certain people I am responsible for staying in touch with, and I keep a record of when I have called them.

Those whom I have seen as a counselor. I even keep a record of reimbursements for services.

Notes of important lectures or summaries of important articles that I have read. Sometimes I will copy significant passages or pithy quotes which have struck me with force.

The back of the journal is for my own material, the productions of my unconscious, my own listening, my own insights, and my own reflections. The front part of the journal is focused on my conscious, directed life and the ideas and inspirations of other people. Here my thinking, organizing, outer self has its say. In one little notebook I

can record both the business of outer life and my interaction with the depths of myself and beyond.

Typing a journal

Some people find that it is easier for them to keep their
inner log by using a typewriter rather than keeping a record in longhand. They can write much faster when they
type, and for them typing interferes less with the creative
process within them. Whatever is the easiest way to keep
at the inner journey is the best way for the particular individual.

I have one friend who gets up in the morning and records
his dreams on a typewriter. He then goes on to do his reflection on the typewriter. He keeps these pages in a loose-
leaf notebook. Another friend does much the same and
keeps the pages in a file until she has a sheaf of them. Then
she places them in a spring binder for a permanent record.

I find that when I take longer times for my inner listening,
for working on specific problems, or for imaginative work,
that the typewriter allows me greater freedom. The typewriter, however, is not always available and cannot be carried with me wherever I go. I would suggest that beginners
start with a composition book and mechanical pencil and
move to a typewriter when they feel this would give them
more freedom of expression.

One of the most important aspects of journal keeping is
the permanence of the record. It is so easy to lose individual
sheets of paper or to throw away jottings we don't like. In
a spiral notebook or a bound composition book one has
to make an effort to tear out the pages one wishes to forget.

Some people ask if they cannot simply speak their journal

WHAT KIND OF JOURNAL?

into a tape recorder. They may have a block which makes it difficult for them to write. There are many disadvantages of a taped journal. Unless one puts such a journal on a computer, there is no easy way of going back through what one has dreamed or reflected without a great expenditure of time. Of course one can type the tapes, but again this takes a lot of time. But if there is no other way that one can keep a journal, tapes are certainly better than nothing at all.

The same basic suggestions for keeping a journal hold for those who type it as for those who use longhand. One way of keeping a sense of continuity when typing is by numbering either the pages or the dreams. This also encourages one to keep the total record. For continuity and availability spiral notebooks have many advantages, and for those who go the typing route I would still suggest that they keep a simple handwritten log as well.

Some do's and don'ts

My journal is written for me and for me alone. If I wish to share it with others (as I will suggest later on), I will usually read it to them. In my case it would be a necessity, as I find it difficult at times to read my own writing. Legibility and neatness are not important to me. As long as the record is decipherable to me using my best intuition, the record is adequate. One should not worry about the way the journal looks or one's handwriting. Spelling, likewise, is of no consequence. All that is necessary is that I know what I mean. The same applies to sentence structure, grammar, punctuation, margins, etc. However, the more you write the easier it is to express yourself, the greater your ability to use words, and the more fun journal keeping is.

Why is it so difficult to make the commitment to take life playfully and seriously and to keep some record of it? One reason mentioned in the first chapter is that we have been conditioned against writing by bad teaching of the reading and writing arts. Our personality can also put up some blocks. An introvert will be more interested in an inner record than an extrovert. The latter is more interested in leaving a record in the outside world. Reading and writing are basically intuitive skills, and they are more difficult for people whose skill and interest lie in dealing with outer concrete realities. Some kind of journal keeping may be particularly helpful for such people, however, as it may encourage them to stop and reflect and put their lives in perspective.

Probably the most important reason most people do not keep a journal is simply that they do not value themselves enough to think their lives worth recording or reflecting on. They feel they cannot write publishable material, and that only this would give their musings any value. When, however, I begin to see the infinite value of every human being (even myself), I am in a certain sense cheating both God and the world when I do not make a reflective, imaginative record of my inner being. I have a place, a value, and a destiny which no other person can fulfill. How can I begin to value myself in this way? This usually requires a radical shift in my view of myself and of the universe of which I am a part.

3

Actually Getting
Started

How do i actually get started in keeping a journal?
Once I have really decided that I want to use a written,
permanent record as a part of my religious journey, how
do I begin?

One of the best ways to start is to write out the reasons
for keeping an inner account of one's life. This writing can
tell you a lot about what you truly believe about the universe and your place in it. It is seldom possible to discover
what you believe until you write it down. It is next to impossible to analyze or criticize what are merely thoughts
in your head. It is much easier to look objectively at your
beliefs once they have been written down in black and
white. What do I really believe about the world in which I
live, about the nature of God, about my relationship with
both? Sometimes I will find that there are several different
views within me which are in conflict with one another. In
that case, which of them is the predominant view in my
life? How does the other one express itself?

At several recent conferences I have suggested that people
draw a picture of their soul and its place in the cosmos. It

was amazing to see the depth of people that this exercise uncovered. We started a summer school session at the Presbyterian School of Religious Education by writing out our world view in two pages. Few of the students had ever tried to state their vision of the world clearly. At the end of the course they wrote another two pages to see how their views had changed. One can only record change as one knows where one was in the beginning.

In order to discover what you believe, you need first of all to set aside at least an hour or two. Ask yourself this question: How do I view the universe and my place in it? Then take up a pencil and see what pours out. If you prefer you can draw the way your soul looks in the world and then describe in words the meaning of what you have drawn. We seldom actually take stock of ourselves. When we write as honestly as we can we may be surprised to find what our basic assumptions and beliefs truly are. We may be startled to discover the principles on which we run our lives.

Another way to begin is to write what you believe the basic message of Jesus of Nazareth is. Is it one that you believe in or want to believe in? Would you like to believe in a love like that of the prodigal Father's? Would you like to experience that kind of love? What kind of program would you undertake in order to come to know that love? How would you change your daily pattern to make a deepening experience of that love possible? Again, unless I write down such a program, the chances are that it will not be realized in concrete action. Writing down a rule, a way of life, or a program commits one to action infinitely more than just thinking about it. It cannot be accomplished in one half-hour daily listening time. This kind of writing will require several hours.

Learning to be silent

Once you have set the stage for keeping a journal by looking at the reason for keeping one, how do you begin a time
of daily reflection and listening? Unless your journal is to
be merely a rehearsal of daily events and ordinary concerns
and anxieties, you need to learn to be still and discover that
there is another dimension of reality. One finds response
from this aspect of the universe once one has become detached from the busyness of everyday life. One of the reasons that I get up in the middle of the night to do my daily
journal writing is that I am already quiet then and do not
have to spend time quieting down.

As long as my mind is raging with thoughts, ideas, plans,
and fears, I cannot listen significantly to God or any other
dimension of reality. In his book *Doors of Perception*
(Harper and Row, 1970), Aldous Huxley suggested that
our sense organs, nervous systems, and brains are basically
eliminative in nature. They are designed to help us survive
on the surface of this particular planet, and so they cut
down or tune out many other possible realms of experience. They rivet our attention on the physical realm and
keep us from being confused and overwhelmed by much
useless and irrelevant information. However, in the process
they keep us out of touch with other dimensions of reality.
We human beings can experience a spiritual dimension as
well as a physical one. In quietness we find detachment and
so untie ourselves from total attention to outer, physical
reality. Then we sometimes find another kind of experience
breaking through. Only those entirely brainwashed by
Western materialism ignore this possibility.

In *The Other Side of Silence* I discuss this matter in much greater depth. It is nearly impossible, however, to begin to listen to the voice of God without first learning to be quiet; and so it is necessary to give some simple instructions on how to be quiet. These are the suggestions I use at conferences when I am leading a group in an exercise in quiet listening.

First of all we need to find a place in which we will not be disturbed. Then we must find a position in which we are comfortable and in which we will not sleep easily. I find that sitting comfortably in an erect position is excellent. The Simontons in their book *Getting Well Again* (Tarcher, 1978), suggest this position. The description in that book of their method of helping cancer patients provides the finest simple set of rules for being quiet that I have encountered anywhere.

Next it is necessary to stop outer action. There is a kind of prayer which can be done while washing the dishes or working in the garden. Total listening to God, on the other hand, requires my total attention.

Having stopped my outer activity, I try to stop my inner thoughts and desires, the movements of the mind and will. This is more difficult. Sometimes saying a simple phrase like "Jesus, mercy" or the Jesus prayer ("Lord Jesus, Son of God, have mercy on me, a sinner") can help one settle down. Roman Catholics may find the "Hail, Mary" useful. Another help is to try to stop my inner talking, not to let myself talk to myself. When talking to myself, I find that the muscles around my voice box move slightly. I am not totally still physically when talking to myself.

As I become still, I begin to think of the things I have left undone, the calls I should have made, the letters I should have written, the jobs I need to do. Sometimes ideas for my writing come to me. I find it helpful to have my journal present and at hand. I can write these things down and tell myself that I will take care of them later. If I try to hold onto these ideas and be still, I effectively destroy any real possibility of becoming truly quiet within.

As I begin to be still I may well become aware of tension in many parts of my body. When I am tense, I am not quiet. Tension is preparation for action, being on guard. Often I may not even realize that I am taut as a rubber band until I take the time to be still. I can then quietly let go of tension, starting with the top of my head, over my face, down my neck, down my arms, down my torso to my legs. This is only necessary when I discover tension within me. Most of us, however, have some tension most of the time; and this exercise is a good one for all of us from time to time.

Most Eastern religions speak of the importance of breathing when trying to be quiet. I cannot be still when I am huffing and puffing like a steam engine. Breathing is the only major bodily function that can be controlled both consciously and unconsciously. Slowing down breathing to seven or eight breaths a minute has a quieting effect on the whole body. Classical Christian writers like the Greek fathers on Mt. Athos and Ignatius of Loyola recommended deep and quiet breathing as an aid to quieting down and meditating.

When some people try to become quiet they fall asleep. If it happens only once in a while, it may indicate insufficient rest and you should enjoy it. You might even have a helpful dream. If it happens often, try various practices to stay awake. The main caution is not to get angry or upset about going to sleep, or you will be lifted right out of your silence.

One of the reasons for recording dreams is that they spring

naturally out of the quietness of sleep and reveal this other dimension of reality. In deep quiet, images and pictures begin to bubble up out of the depths of the self. When this occurs you have entered consciously into the realm where dreams occur. Together with alpha brain waves, this is a sign that you are truly quiet. You can turn inward and follow these images. Indeed, one kind of meditation involves following these images and trying to understand them and their meaning.

Many people find that being quiet with others helps them quiet down and become silent. An atmosphere of quiet engenders quiet. One cannot always depend on others for coming into quietness. But periods of quietness with others in a prayer group can help in establishing ways to come to an inner calm.

As you conclude your daily time of quiet and listening, take three or four minutes to move from the quiet back into the ordinary world. In the middle of the night you do not need this threshhold time, but can rather go back into the deeper quiet of sleep.

Listening to the inner guide

I remember clearly how I began to listen in silence. I had come to a dead-end street. I was talking to a Jewish Jungian analyst. We were discussing my inability to sleep at night. I would awaken after three or four hours of sleep and then be unable to go back to sleep again, and I wondered how I could carry on through a busy day with this kind of tiredness. My counselor, Max Zeller, asked me if I had any idea why I couldn't sleep. I didn't. He suggested it might be that God wanted to talk with me. When I showed my complete skepticism at such an idea, he said: "God woke up Samuel to get his message to him. Why do you think he will not speak to you? Has God changed?"

If one is hurting enough one will do something as foolish as getting up in the middle of the night to listen to the depths. The following night when I awoke I got up and went to a place where I could be warm. With journal and pencil in hand, I spoke inwardly: "Well, God, here I am, what do you have on your mind?" To my utter amazement something spoke back to me. I recorded both the questions and the answers. We had quite a conversation, and these conversations have continued nearly every night during the past 28 years. Each one is different, but they are variations on one theme. Out of them have come great clarity in seeing what is amiss within me and an impetus toward change within my life. In them I have been moved to efforts of restitution, forgiveness, and love. Out of these times of nightly dialog have come most of the ideas for my sermons, articles, and books. They have been a wellspring of life and wisdom for me.

The first attempt nearly 30 years ago went something like this:

Well, Lord, here I am. A friend told me that I should come here in the middle of the night and ask you what you have on your mind. Are you there? Do you wish to talk with me? You know that I need my sleep.

I want you, my child, and want to help you become what you are capable of becoming. I love you and want to give you that love.

Why don't you do it at a more reasonable time, during the day or in the evening?

I can never get your attention then. You are so busy that if I am to break through with love and concern for you I must make you uncomfortable and get to you in the middle of the night when you wouldn't think of doing anything else.

If it hadn't been for Max Zeller, I would never have understood the message. I might have gone down the drain. That hardly seems like kindness and concern.

Just because you have forgotten how to listen to the depth is no reason that I am not who I am. It is not really my fault that you have not heard the message of Scripture and the church. I am always here and seeking your fellowship. You have been so caught up with the outer world and your own ideas that you have forgotten the reality of the inner world.

Why do you want me? I am of no value. You must know all my faults and lusts and angers. How could you love me?

Child, child, how little you understand. I am love. I can no more help loving you and all human beings than the leopard can change his spots. It is my nature to love and I have created all human beings because I wanted to love them and have them respond to me. I long for them to stop and receive my love.

You mean that you can care for me? Me, with all my stupidity, anger, self-will, egotism?

That is the whole point of my being. I would have died for you if you had been the only human being. It is your very need for me which makes my love flow even more. Those who are getting along well don't need my love as much as those who are lost and struggling and in pain.

If you really care for me and if you are really there, I don't have to do it all on my own. I don't have to be afraid.

That is right, but before this day is over, you will forget this conversation, this encounter, and chalk it up to illusion. You will get busy and forget.

What then would you have me do?

Have the courage to come back each night and get restored. Have the discipline to get up and talk with me even if you lose your sleep. Then during the day pause and remember that I am with you and will help you through the day. Seek me before you make any decisions or take important actions. Remember that I

*am here and I love you and that since I have conquered even
death, you don't have to fear anything, even death.*

I'll try to come back and I will try to remember. Help me,
Lord.

Each person will find that the Spirit of God will speak to
him or to her according to their needs, in terms of their
problems. Sometimes the Spirit within gives clear evidence
of a knowledge and wisdom beyond our own. A Catholic
priest friend was very active in the charismatic renewal. He
was afraid that the bishop would not accept his place within
the movement or the movement itself. I suggested that he
take his journal and write. The conversation he had was
incredibly supportive and told him exactly what the bishop's
reaction would be, a reaction which had never occurred to
him to hope for. The next day in his meeting with the bishop everything occurred just as his inner dialog had predicted
and he was duly impressed.

It is really astounding how many people who say that they
believe in prayer do not really believe that it is a two-way
street and that God can respond to our needs, our questions, our fears, our doubts. It is helpful to have a record of
this to look back on and reflect on. If I simply have this
record in my head and do not write it in my journal, it is
too easy to dismiss the entire encounter as wishful thinking.
It is much more difficult to dismiss the pencil marks on a
piece of paper, particularly when they have spoken the truth
about us and the world around us.

We can easily forget these conversations. As I look back
over my journal I am impressed by the reality and power of
these encounters. They have had a greater and more lasting
impact on me than all but the most important outer events.

It is difficult to give a picture of the variety of conversations that can take place, and some of the conversations are far too personal to share. The important thing is to find a time to be still and open yourself to the inner Christ and allow yourself to receive his wisdom, concern, and love. If, indeed, such a relationship is possible and I still do not take the time to have such a conversation, I am saying in effect one of two things. Either I do not believe that it is possible to have such a relationship with spiritual reality, or else I do not need or want such a relationship. What I do is a better indication of what I truly believe than what I say or think I believe. Keeping a journal is a way of testing the hypothesis that God is self-sacrificing love, is available and wants to have a relationship with me and share his love with me.

Let me give you another example, a very recent conversation. This one occurred in the early hours of the morning after I had had enough sleep. I did this before I took up any outer duties and activities.

Here I am, Lord, angry and hurt and peevish. Life seems difficult and devoid of all joy. Even you seem far off. There seems to be nothing but work, work, work. I've had some good days, but it seems as though I am always living on the edge of an abyss. It seems like no one understands me or appreciates me.

Come and let us talk. I hear another voice speaking in you, in addition to your own. You have fallen into listening to the destructive voice which nearly always lies to some extent. How can you possibly say that no one appreciates you? One of your problems is that too many people do, and they overwhelm you with too much mail, too many phone calls, and too many demands on your time.

How did I fall into the hands of that dark voice again? What did I do?

The further you go and the more you speak of me and love, the more the dark one is going to try to undermine you and get your attention. Once you have been opened to the inner world, you must continue on the journey. There is no standing still. It is either going forward or falling back into the hands of the dark one. Sensitivity is being open to the depth of the spiritual realm. It means that your ego is not encased in steel. The seed has cracked its husk and the plant must either grow or die.

At times I get very sick and tired of growing. I just want to stop all this inner work. I'm weary.

I understand your weariness. Remember, I endured the cross. There is much evil in the world, and the evil one exploits the hatred and pettiness and selfishness and lust of human beings to the hilt. That is why you need to come back here and be refreshed, come back to the spring, the source.

I'm so afraid that you will drop me. I know that this is irrational. I know that you have supported and protected me in a thousand different situations.

Come to me and let me hold you until the fear subsides. Come to the secret garden where the sun is shining, the grass is green, the flowers are blooming. From the rocky cliffs the waters of life spring forth, falling into a pool of crystal water and then flowing in a stream down to the sea. Come rest your head upon my breast and be refreshed. Wash in the waters, and be cleansed and renewed.

We come to this place in which we have met many times before. It is for me a sanctuary like the one described by St. John of the Cross in his poem, *The Dark Night*. He writes there of the castle with its turrets and the breezes blowing through the cedars. In my meditation the Lord and I go to this secret place where we have met before. I rest for a while and then we begin to talk again.

What would you have me do, Lord?

Rise up and go out and give to others the love and care I have given you. Let my love reveal and heal your hurts. Try not to be peevish and angry with those closest to you. Remember that I am with you. Remember also that as you give way to nastiness and self-pity you throw yourself into the hands of the dark one.

Thank you, Lord, for this time with you. I will try to rise up and go your way. Help me to stay in your presence and be with me throughout this day.

Few things have been more helpful and supportive to me than these daily turnings inward to listen. Sometimes the conversations are much shorter. Here is another shorter example of an early morning encounter from a few days ago:

I awake from a good night's sleep; dreams are just beyond the edge of recall. In my mind as I awake is the thought that I'll change my schedule or my life any way that you wish. I don't have to be set in cement. Then comes the realization that I live on the edge of an abyss and that when I am too busy I fall into this abyss. I speak; what do you want, Lord?

Keep reflecting, and don't push yourself too hard. Also don't feel afraid of a little tiredness. You may not need as much sleep as you thought. You drove yourself too hard yesterday.

What do I do?

Experiment with various plans, don't get caught up in one. I am with you. You don't have to finish this book by the 4th or 5th of January. Life is really going well for you. Stay close to me and my love. You are in a beautiful spot with one who truly loves you. I am here also. What more do you want?

I want to feel happy and contented all the time. Help me not to go into a snit when life is not exactly what I want it to be. I dread the next two lecturing trips.

Let go and flow with the current of my life and love. Have fun this day and see what the day brings.

I'll try.

At times we meet problems in these daily encounters that cannot be handled in the 30 or 40 minutes allotted for that conversation. There are many different ways of dealing with the moods and attitudes which emerge within us.

Some of my friends share their journals with me. A

brother in a religious order who does counseling recently
shared the following passage. I know him well and what
came to him in this conversation spoke to his very deepest
need and seemed to be a genuine experience of God.

Jesus, I feel so responsible for others because I touch interior
parts of them. I need a break. I need to be loved.
You are a good person, John.
Jesus, something in me doubts that and sabotages my confidence within me.
*Fight it, John. Don't go gentle—fight it. You are stronger
than you realize. The inner darkness can overwhelm. I want
you to learn the objective nature of evil, outside and within. It
will attack you in your weakest area, but there you are also
strongest. Fight it with me. Say to it: "No. Begone, evil." I tell
you, if you speak in my name and with faith, you have what I
the Lord God almighty have given you, my strength. You must
win with me. Behold, I have not given you the spirit of fear, but
of power and love and of a sound mind. John, please be my
friend and fight it. Otherwise I cannot work through you as
effectively as I desire. You are to be a channel of love for me,
and this fear you must overcome. I cannot do it for you. Please
be courageous. Know, John, that I love you and that I am with
you; and the only way that we can be deeper friends is if we are
parallel, if we work together. Fight the deceiver. I give you my
strength. You must do your part. Behold, John, I have given
you strength.*

The value of conversations of this kind can hardly be over-
estimated. Rosalind Rinker has written clearly and simply
about prayer as conversation in her book, *Prayer: Conversing with God* (Zondervan, 1971). However, she does not
suggest recording these encounters. How much more real
and permanent these conversations become when they are
written out!

4

The Journal
as Symbol of My
Unique Value

ONE EXCELLENT WAY of overcoming resistance to regular journal usage is to ask the following questions: What are the ten deepest hungers of my heart? What are the ten most troublesome doubts that plague my faith?

I have been asking these questions of those attending my lectures in all sections of the country. Three hungers have emerged as by far the most common: to know God, to feel God's love, and to experience real love and intimacy with other human beings. There is a hunger in the human heart to know the sense of worth which only human and divine love can bring. Two doubts surface as the most common: How can I be sure that there is meaning in this material world? And if there is a central meaning and purpose in the universe, how is it that there is so much evil and suffering in the world?

One reason why it is so difficult for many modern people to believe in the healing ministry of Jesus and the church is that they do not believe there is a loving God who can or wishes to heal. I will never forget speaking on Christian healing before a group many years ago. The wife of a Pres-

byterian minister came up to me after the talk and said she
had never heard of anything like that. She knew that God
could bring disaster and tragedy, but she had not considered
the idea that his caring could bring healing in this 20th
century.

Francis McNutt often speaks in lectures of the inhuman
way that many people view God. He has said that we would
put a father in jail who said to a disobedient child: "Since
you have been naughty I will give you a little leukemia."
And yet we treat God as if he would punish us in this way.
No one with good sense would want to keep a record of
one's relationship with such a being. One would keep an account of one's encounters with a God of this nature only to
learn how to placate him and avoid him. Most of us would
rather not deal with him at all.

The way I view the universe in which I live determines
whether I keep a journal and what kind of a journal I keep.
There are basically only a few different ways to understand
the cosmos in which we live.

If I see the world as essentially meaningless, I have only
one reason for keeping a journal. It is a stubborn protest in
the face of the gale. Confronting either a physical world of
random atoms and bubbling mud pots or a spiritual world
of meaningless spiritual elements, I can only scream out in
defiance at the absurdity of it all. My very rebellion will
disintegrate and be lost, but I rage none the less. Fortunately,
only a few people keep journals under these circumstances.
It is easier to eat, drink, and be merry and forget the pain of
it all in drugs, alcohol, sex, and busyness. Journal keeping
in a meaningless world is an act of heroic defiance, and
there aren't many defiant heroes.

Many primitive peoples believe in gods and goddesses,

but these are seen as essentially hostile and destructive, and they begrudge human beings any joy or happiness (few Hindus want to fall into the hands of the gods Shiva or Kali). If one's life is spent in hiding from malevolent deities and demons, there is no reason to leave a record; the less record one leaves, the better.

Some believe the forces of the universe are not hostile, but ambivalent. They believe that if they treat them properly, they may get by. Only respectful people have value, and then only as long as the deity continues to think favorably of them. The god is seen in the image of an oriental potentate, whom one watches with a cautious eye and before whom one grovels upon one's belly. His fiat is law; his subjects have no value in themselves.

Sometimes Yahweh appears in this light. When God met Moses after the experience of the burning bush and tried to kill him (Exod. 4:24), or when Uzzah was struck dead after touching the ark (2 Sam. 6:3-8), he seemed hardly friendly. If God is seen as parceling out the miseries described in Deut. 28:15-68, then human beings have value only when they are good. Given the faulty record of most of us, this passage does not encourage most men and women to seek out God. Under these circumstances human life seems hardly important enough to record.

There is, however, quite a different strand in the Old Testament that anticipates the view of Jesus. In the writings of Hosea we see the love relationship of Yahweh with the people of Israel acted out in a dramatic way. Some of the psalmists sang of a tender and loving God. It takes some sophistication to be able to pick and choose among these various elements within the Old Testament. At one veterans hospital for the mentally ill, the chaplains—Jewish, Catholic, and Protestant—agreed that it was not wise to circulate the Old Testament within the wards. Without interpretation it could easily be misunderstood.

An ambivalent deity is harder to deal with than a hostile one. An ambivalent parent does more damage than a harsh and consistently angry one. Few things devalue human life more than the ambivalence of those close to us. When a parent or sister, child or friend is affectionate one day, angry another, and then cold and distant, we do not know how to respond. The same is true of God.

The view of the divine provided by Buddhism and Hinduism has become more and more popular in the West in recent years. It is certainly more attractive than most of the views we have already described. Within this vision of reality the physical world is an illusion. History is an illusion. Concrete and unique human beings are illusions. The goal of life is to rid one's self of illusion and to merge into the cosmic mind, sometimes described as nothingness and sometimes as bliss. This journey requires great effort and enlightenment. Since concrete, physical individuals are only a passing expression of eternal reality, the unique experiences and thoughts of ordinary people have little value. According to this point of view, one's uniqueness needs to be lost rather than emphasized by keeping a journal.

God as divine lover

There is still another view of the universe which is supremely revealed by Jesus of Nazareth. In this view the center and core of reality is not the cosmic mind with which one merges as one divests one's self of uniqueness and personality. Rather, the central organizing principle which has made the world and human beings is pure unbounded love, a prodigal father who is always reaching out to us human beings no matter how silly, stupid, or malicious we are or might have been. This is the good news, news so good that few humans believe it. Certainly this God was not made in the human image. Few of us have ever known such love. What we long for in our deepest heart of hearts is exactly the one Jesus described as *Abba,* "Daddy." This God wishes to give us love and transformation, intimacy and healing care. In order to understand the importance of this idea for Christian journal keeping it is necessary for us to describe Jesus' knowledge of God.

Jesus effectively conveyed the radical meaning of this idea in one of his absurd stories. If we think the story of the prodigal father is absurd in our day, we have only a faint glimmering of how ridiculous it was in Jesus' time. Kenneth Bailey lived most of his life in the Near East, and in his book *The Cross and the Prodigal* (Concordia, 1973) he looks at this story from the point of view of the customs of that region. These customs have changed little in the 2000 years since this story was first told.

A man had two sons. It would not surprise most of us if our son or daughter came home for supper one evening and told us, "It's dull at home. I want my share of the inheritance so I can go do what I want." But in the village life of the Middle East such behavior would be unthinkable. It would be like a son telling his father, "I wish you were dead." Even more unthinkable would be the father's response, for giving the son his share of the property would work hardship on those who remained. And what would the other villagers think of such an extravagant action! The property would bring only a small part of its value when the son turned it quickly into gold. This father's actions made no sense.

Once the son had his cash in hand he probably headed for some Gentile city, perhaps Antioch. Antioch was known as a city in which every vice flourished. There the son spent his money in wine, women, and song. He would have gone to the Roman bath, which can best be described as a three-dimensional pornographic film.

After breaking nearly every provision of the moral law, his money gave out and there was a famine. He then broke the ritual law as well. To keep body and soul together he hired himself out to tend pigs, and he was so hungry that he would have gladly eaten the pods which the swine ate. It is difficult to imagine the abhorrence this detail would have aroused in Jewish hearers of the story. Contact with pigs carried something of the same quality as adultery did in 18th-century Boston.

Finally the young man came to his senses. I have never been too impressed with his conversion. His stomach pinched and he thought to himself: "The hired servants at home do better than this. I know what I will do. I will get up and go home and tell my father that I have sinned against heaven and earth and am no longer worthy to be called his son and ask to be made one of the hired servants." I do not see any great transformation of character in this desire to go home. And the son still had little understanding of the true nature of his father.

Evidently the father went out each day to sit in the shade of a tree and scan the horizon, looking and hoping for his son's return. One day in the far distance he saw a speck, and even at that distance the eyes of love knew who it was. He literally dashed out to meet his son. The Greek word which is used is the same one used for running a race in the arena. Middle Eastern householders don't act like that! He would have had to pull up his long alb-like garment, and his underwear might have shown!

He ran to his son and embraced him before his son knew what had happened. He had been trudging along the path head down, and then this embrace—but he knew that embrace. In the chapel at the University of Notre Dame there is on one side of the high altar a Mestrovic bronze of the prodigal son with his head buried in the father's breast; on the other side is a monumental marble of the Pieta, the crucified Jesus lying in his mother's arms. One statue represents the story Jesus told, and the other is the story he lived.

The son automatically began his little speech, but his father didn't even let him finish. Instead he called to his servants and told them to bring shoes, the best robe in the house, and a ring for his son.

These gifts were significant. Of course, the boy needed shoes, for his feet were bloody. They were not the calloused feet of a hired man. But the shoes signified far more than that. Shoes separated householders from servants. The father was welcoming his son back into the home *not* as a servant, but as a son.

The boy needed a robe. He was naked from the waist up, but why the best robe? Certainly an ordinary homespun cloak would have been good enough for this wastrel. The best robe of Damascus silk was yet another sign to everyone of how much the father loved his son. It was an outward and visible sign of his forgiveness and overflowing love. Everyone could tell what the father thought by this gift.

But the ring—this was too much. Here was the son who had wasted the family substance in riotous living. He had

had his share of the property. The ring was something the son did not need. It was pure grace. It may have been just another sign of the father's total acceptance of the son, or it may have been even more, as Kenneth Bailey suggests. The word used for the ring is the same one used to describe the signet ring of ancient times, which was used to sign documents. The Chinese use symbols in much the same way today in their use of a pictogram or chop. Possession of this ring made the son a legal member of the family again. In every way the son was reintegrated into the very fabric of the family.

And then the father ordered a great feast, a banquet with dancing and music, with wine and the best foods. I am not sure that as a returned prodigal I would have looked forward to meeting all the servants and friends of the family at such a party. What would I say when they asked me where I had been? Such is the price of humility that prodigals have to pay.

The father's embrace in this story Jesus told foreshadowed the ministry of the healing touch in the early church. This banquet foreshadowed the eucharistic feast. Several years ago I was lecturing in Schloss Craheim in Bavaria. One group had been studying Jesus' use of symbols. For our final evening together this group presented the story of the prodigal in pantomime. When 90 educated Germans gather together there are enough musical instruments for a concert orchestra, and so excellent music accompanied the movements of the actors. At the moment when the father ordered the feast, the great doors opening into the central hall of the castle were thrown open. Tables laden with bread and fruit and wine were brought in, and we partook of the Eucharist. This central service of the Christian church is provided to receive all prodigals who come home to the Father for whatever reason.

And this is not the end of the story. There was another son. He had been working hard in the fields, perhaps too hard. He may have been a workaholic. He heard the music and saw the many burning torches, and he sent a servant to see what had happened now to his addled father. When he discovered that the party was for his returned brother, he was arrogant and spiteful, and he would not go in. If it had been inappropriate for a father to give away his property and then welcome the wastrel home again, it was even more inappropriate for him to leave such a party to go out and plead with the other son who had refused to come in. The younger son had been stupid and headstrong. The elder son was now insolent, yet the father went out and begged him to come back in and be glad that his brother had returned to the bosom of the family.

A journal is an instrument by which both prodigals and elder brothers can turn inward, reflect, and come home. Those of us who are more often like the younger brother can use a journal for reflection and so get up from our swine swill and come home. The elder brothers among us can use a friendly journal to see how little we have appreciated our Father's love and how much of the burden of our work is self-imposed. Having looked at our reflection in the mirror of a journal, we can laugh at ourselves, come to the party, and taste the joy of the heavenly banquet.

The essential Christian message

Mary Stewart has written two delightful novels about Merlin and King Arthur. In *The Crystal Cave* (Fawcett,

1979) she tells the story of the young Merlin who was raised to think of himself as a despised bastard, only to discover later that he was the king's son. He found his way to the king and was received by him with love. In *The Hollow Hills* (Fawcett, 1979) she tells the story of yet another youth who discovered the same truth, none other than King Arthur himself. These stories touch a very deep level within us, because in a real sense we are all king's sons and daughters who do not realize our heritage. We need to discover who we are and find our way home. A journal is a guidebook in which we can begin to realize who we are and how to get home to the Father's love.

One we have recognized this love as the central message of Jesus we can begin to hear how it sings through the entire gospel narrative through parable, discourse, and action. The healing ministry is primarily a ministry of this love, as I have pointed out in my book, *Healing and Christianity* (Harper and Row, 1976). Jesus heals because the kingdom of God is breaking through his life and touching the aching hurt of humankind. The story which Jesus lived was far more dramatic than the story that he told. His death and resurrection give reason to believe the story he told. Jesus, as God incarnate, came among men and women and reached out to us even before we had come far enough by ourselves to start home. He died for us to show his love and rescue all people from the darkness and confusion in which we had been lost. Paul put it clearly and well in his letter to the Romans: "But God has shown us how much he loves us— it was while we were still sinners that Christ died for us! . . . We were God's enemies, but he made us his friends through the death of his Son" (Rom. 5:8, 10 TEV).

Throughout the history of the church some men and

women have caught the depth and truth of this love. They have tried to let that love flow through them, and when it has shown through them we call them saints. The essential characteristic, the common denominator of sainthood is that individuals have heard the message of God's love and respond to it by loving other human beings as God has loved them. This is true of them all: Ambrose, Catherine of Genoa, Francis of Assisi, Mother Julian of Norwich, Florence Nightingale, and Paul himself.

Relating to a loving Father

It is very different for a small child or returning prodigal (or even an elder brother) to approach a loving father than it is to approach a stern and demanding father. And this is very different from coming before a judge, no matter how righteous, who will hold us responsible for all that we have done and make us pay for our misdeeds. It is also very different from the way we would approach a despotic, ambivalent, unpredictable oriental monarch.

It is impossible for me as a human father to give love to a child who views me with suspicion, dislike, and fear—a child who expects punishment and rejection. There is no way I can effectively give love to my children until they trust me enough to tell me what they feel and let down their guard with me. For many years there was a wall between one of my sons and me. Finally he was able to express his dislike of me, his doubts and fears. I did not reject him or criticize him. A real friendship developed between us, and I could begin to share the depth of my caring for him. I could love him as he was, not expecting him to be what I wanted him to be. Sometime later I was with him in my own need and he could share his love freely and deeply with me.

Exactly the same truth applies to our relationship with God. He cannot give me the love I desire until I trust him enough to bring all of myself and so realize that he can love all of me. I never know the depth of God's love until I bring all of me again and again and again. God cannot by his very nature give me the love he desires to give me until I approach him as the loving Father that he is. Only in relationship to him can I begin to grow into that loving being I am capable of becoming.

A journal is one important place where I can gather all of me together to bring my total being before God. It is the place where I test the hypothesis that God loves me as a prodigal Father. It is the laboratory in which I test out the reality of God's love. In the New Testament all Christians are referred to as saints. Ordinary Christians who try to open their inner beings to God can come into the same relationship with him as the saints we have already mentioned. God wants to give us his love. It is often impossible for partly conscious, educated modern men and women to bring the totality of themselves before God without using a journal.

Actions speak much louder than words. Let us imagine that we have an elderly parent living with us at home. We profess that we love this parent very much. And yet when we come home in the evening after being out all day at work, we do not stop in to see him or her for a moment. We do not stop by to see our parent in his or her room after dinner or before we go to work in the morning. We really do not care much about that person, no matter what we may say. A journal provides an occasion to stop in our busy life and spend some time with the heavenly Father. As I spend more and more time I bring more and more of my life and thoughts to him. And I begin to know more and more what real love is about.

Appreciating my own value

Only one experience gives value to us fragile men and women: being loved. And there is only one way I know of to have confidence that my value goes beyond this moment and continues in the life to come: coming to know and experience the incredible love of the heavenly Father who has created this universe, both spiritual and physical, and still holds it in his hand.

A journal helps us toward this realization and is also a record of our unique experience of this love. In his book *Exercises in Religious Understanding* (Notre Dame, 1975), David Burrell has pointed out that the *Confessions* of St. Augustine would have been impossible in any view of the world other than the one expressed by Jesus of Nazareth. The *Confessions* were a new kind of writing in which the individual had supreme value, and all which brings that individual to God is significant. It is also significant that the *Confessions* are a journal of this great fourth century sinner turned saint, of a prodigal returned home.

The idea that I have unique, eternal value is a radical one. That God himself would come on a rescue operation and die and rise again to bring human beings to the fulfillment of their value is beyond the imagination of most people. Such a belief does not rise often in ordinary men and women. They have to learn it from someone or someplace. In my journal I can record where and how I first began to understand this truth about the universe.

We don't lock students who are trying to learn integral calculus in a room and tell them to stay there until they have come up with what it is. We teach them. And one of the main tasks of the church is to teach people about this incredible love of God. Few people come up with this vision of the universe by themselves. Some may have an imaginative intuition that something like this might be possible, but such mystical visions convince few people. But the church proclaims that God stepped into the pages of history, and that we have a record of his action in the New Testament. The purpose of the church is to live out and spread this message. The community of Christians must be doing both if it is really to do either. Such a community of like-minded people is needed to truly live out the inner journey toward that love.

It is so easy to go off the track religiously. I need some time-tried institution in which I can learn and grow, in which I can talk to others and test my relationship with God and other human beings. Churches are human institutions. This is unfortunate in that their mistakes and misunderstandings injure some people. But it is fortunate in that it shows how much God trusts us human beings to express his love.

In my journal I can reflect on my relationship to my church and to other Christian groups. I can pause and consider the problems and graces I find in my church. For those who have nothing to do with churches because they are so filled with hypocrites, I would remind them that there is always room for one more. Journal musing about one's church experience will help show one how to receive and give the most within this fallible institution. Your journal can be your intimate companion and confidante as you look for and live in a church in which the inner quest can be understood and pursued. This kind of reflective church membership can be creative both for you as an individual and for the institution. C. S. Lewis' *Screwtape Letters* (Revell, 1978) is in reality such a journal.

A journal also encourages us to think creatively. It is no easy matter to fit the God of love whom I have been describing into this dog-eat-dog world in which most of us live. One has to have a belief in a spiritual world as well as in physical reality and a theory of good and evil. There is no better way of checking one's thinking than writing out what one believes. I know of no substitute for a journal in helping me do this. It is also difficult to share my convictions about God's love unless I can clearly describe what I believe to myself.

A real and continuing relationship to a God of love, to the prodigal Father, requires that I give to others what I receive from him. I cut myself off from God when I do not allow that love to flow through me to others. *My relationship with God (and this is what my Christian meditation is about) is never complete until some other human being feels more loved by me.* As other people learn something about the love of God through my love, they can then turn and find it for themselves. In my deepest relationships with other human beings I sometimes experience the reality and presence of the God who dwells within them. In such relationships it is almost as if God were communing with himself, using two human beings as channels. This is the ultimate in mystical experience.

A diagram may help. In the following diagram the right-

hand triangle represents the totality of myself in touch
with both the physical and nonphysical aspects of reality.
I am in touch with evil and good in both. The message
begins in the church represented in the center. I turn inward to discover and verify that love of Christ of which I
have been told. After encountering and experiencing the
reality of that love, I find myself compelled by gratitude to
share that love with some other specific human being as un-
worthy of my love as I am of Christ's love. When God's
love through "A" finally is accepted in the life of "B," then
"B" can go on to experience further the reality of this love
directly. "B" then seeks those to whom he or she can give of
what he or she has found, and so the reality of the Christian
experience of love is spread.

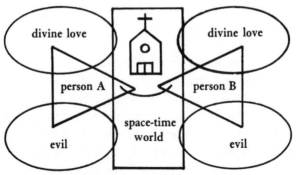

A journal can help in charting one's experience through
these various stages and in giving encouragement and hope
along the way.

The physical world with actual human beings is real and
valuable. What I do concretely and specifically has value.
My actual written journal is a concrete act of love toward
myself. It can be the important record of the occasion of my
turning to God and also of my attempt to bring all of my-

self back to the embrace of the prodigal Father. Likewise a journal is sacramental in that it is an act of love and response to the Father. It is saying to God, "I love you enough to come and relate to you." It is also a chart of my progress in allowing God to love me and allowing the divine love to pass through me to other human beings.

More than a journal

One of the problems that hinders many people in using a journal is the idea that keeping a journal is all that is necessary for a full life. For some writers on the subject, a journal becomes a panacea. They suggest that all one has to do is open one's self to the journal process and all will be well. Everything necessary will happen. I personally doubt that the journal process is enough for most people. Indeed, getting to the depths through a journal can be dangerous unless the journal keeping is part of a larger and more comprehensive practice, and unless one is the type of person who is meant to go the inner way. Not everyone is.

A journal will reflect one's total life. If one's life is directed toward reality, that life will grow and develop. But if the complex of one's outer activities and inner life have no direction or are directed in a destructive and egocentric way, a journal can record disaster. One can read of such disasters in *The Diary of Vaslav Nijinsky* (Univ. of Calif., 1968) or in the last, tragic, rambling writings of Friedrich Nietzsche.

A Christian journal is only part of a process, not the whole process. In order to use a journal as part of the process of being found by God, it is necessary to take a look at the whole. It is to that total process that we now turn.

5

The Process
of Spiritual Growth

Watching a redwood seed germinate and begin its growth into a magnificent, towering tree strikes me with awe. That tiny seed has the potential for incredible development and growth. A human soul has potential for even greater growth in this life and unending growth in the life to come. There are many elements which cooperate to bring about the unfolding of the potential within the seed. The process of transformation of the life hidden in the husk of a seed into a tree offers a picture of the growth process which is possible in a human soul.

We often take growth for granted and forget the complex process of development involved in any living thing. As we consider the many different, separate factors contributing to the growth of any plant, we can better understand the many necessary elements in our human growth toward God and our full potential. In *The Other Side of Silence* I have described this process in detail and refer interested readers to the longer discussion found there.

In order for growth to begin, one must have a living seed, intact and healthy. Likewise for human growth one must begin with an essentially whole, human child endowed with a healthy soul, mind, and body. If the brain or sense organs are impaired beyond a certain point, there is little one can do to help that individual develop. We do not know all the causes producing autistic children or childhood psychosis, but in such cases there is little one can do to bring the person to full development. I admire those who work with these mentally or physically handicapped children or adults, for in such people they do not have the satisfaction of seeing normal development. The process I am describing requires a solid and healthy human who does not have to be protected from the stresses and strains of normal, difficult human development.

Cracking the husk and reaching for the soil

If the seed is ever to be anything but a seed, it must have moisture. Water swells the inner pulp so that it breaks out of potentiality into actuality. This breaking through the husk is necessary to unlock its inner life. Breaking the husk is rebirth into a new dimension. We have already mentioned that this breaking out of the familiar and opening into new dimensions of consciousness is often not a pleasant process. To be opened to one's total environment, physical and spiritual, can be a frightening experience. Primitive societies provide rituals to help growing men and women through these stages. These rites of passage are sometimes brutal and cruel. It is difficult in our society to provide such experiences without being sadistic or even demonic.

On the whole our society provides no methods to help individuals move from childhood to adolescence, from youth to manhood or womanhood, from active life to retirement, or from old age through death. And yet it is difficult for human beings to pass through these various stages without help. Sometimes we fail to make the next step and do not reach our potential.

Using a journal can well be one of the instruments in our modern time for breaking out of our former patterns and beginning to grow in new ways. A journal can help individuals open up to new kinds of experiences and new understandings of the total environment, personal, physical, and spiritual. A journal can also be a comfort as one passes through these difficult stages of growth and transformation.

Because a journal can provide the moisture to crack the husk, it should be used carefully, particularly by young people and people in crisis. *It should never be forced on anyone. One should not require or even encourage other people to penetrate into the depths of their inner being unless the other person is personally attracted to the process.* One should always pay careful attention when someone has the feeling that this way is not for them. Certain personality types may not be attracted to this way. For others it may be wrong. A journal is an instrument which I should only use when I feel called to use it. The initiative for inner probing should nearly always come from the human being wishing it. I will discuss the dangers of journal keeping in the next chapter.

The seed may be healthy and germinate, but if there is no soil into which it can sink its roots, it will soon wither and die. If there is no air into which it can stretch its branches it will not live for long. The human soul cannot begin to grow into the fullness and depth and richness of which it is capable if it does not have both a spiritual and physical environment in which to grow. In the West during the past three or four centuries we have come to believe that only the physical environment is real. Morals and progress and concrete caring are very important, but the soul is seen as only a by-product of the physical human being. Any idea of the soul growing in relationship to a nonphysical or spiritual environment is simply not considered. There can be little soul culture within such a point of view.

In the religious thinking of the East the physical world is on the whole seen as illusory. There is a great deal of wisdom available within this tradition concerning the relation of the soul or psyche to the spiritual world. There is, however, little interest in dealing with the outer world or other human beings, and little belief or action toward changing the outer physical world so that it can be a better place in which humans can live and grow.

Human beings are likely to be stunted unless they believe in the reality of both these worlds. Most Westerners are brought up to *assume* that there is no spiritual world. They cannot conceive of it. It is nearly impossible to take one's spiritual development seriously unless one believes that there is such a domain with which one can interact and in which one can find eternal life. What one does not even imagine as possible, one very seldom takes seriously. This is not the place to show the evidence for the reality of a spiritual world. I have tried to do this in *Encounter with God* (Bethany, 1972) and *Myth, History and Faith* (Paulist, 1974).

If one is to break out of the commonly-accepted materialistic point of view, one needs to do some first-class thinking. I have discovered that new insights which students have are often lost and seldom integrated until they have recorded them in their own words. As one begins to get a new vision of a larger universe it is valuable to write these insights simply for one's self. What we cannot record in simple words is seldom truly understood or believed.

Unless one breaks out of the straightjacket of materialism, one's journal will record little more than the events of the outer world and ephemeral thoughts and fantasies of the human mind. At the same time a journal is an incalculable aid in helping one begin to see the reality of this other dimension. Recording religious experiences and dreams—experiences which seem to reach beyond ordinary sensory data—begins to show the reality of this other dimension. Once one has ventured to try the hypothesis that there may be a spiritual reality with which we can deal, one's journal becomes the laboratory in which to test and verify this hypothesis. A journal also enables us to accumulate the data, and so gives us confidence to explore further. A journal can also keep us from being overwhelmed by this realm when we meet it. Writing down inner encounters gives us ground on which to stand. A journal can also be a place in which we relate our experiences in the spiritual realm to the practical concerns of the workaday world. Indeed, immersing ourselves in the spiritual world without a sense of being concretely in the physical world and keeping some kind of concrete record can be dangerous, as we can get lost in the spiritual realm. In *The Still Point* (Harper and Row, 1971), William Johnston describes how some students of Zen in Japan get lost in *makyō*, which is the world of images, and thus become mentally ill. A journal is one safeguard against this danger.

Light and human warmth

This danger of Zen leads us to the next necessary ingredient for either seed or soul growth. The seed germinates and sinks its roots into the friendly and nurturing soil. A plant begins to grow. Unless there is light, the plant soon withers and dies. Light activates the chlorophyll and provides continuing energy and life for the plant.

If the soul is to grow out of its embryonic first stages it too needs light, the light of divine love. This love can be mediated through human beings. People are like secondary or artificial sources of light. If they are to come to the full possibilities of their humanness, they need to be exposed to divine love.

A journal is an invaluable aid in developing these exposures to God. It is like a photograph in which we can see the light of the divine still shining long after the experience. Likewise the practice of keeping an inner diary can bring us to the time of quiet in which we can be aware of the light. The journal can provide both the occasion for the exposure and its preservation.

The developing plant can be provided with all these things and still not grow. If it is 50 degrees below zero there will be little or no growth. The plant needs warmth. Usually the plant also needs an environment of other plants and animals to help it come to maturity.

In the same way, human beings cannot come to their potential without other human beings. Studies of children who were brought up by animals show clearly that such children are hardly human at all. Language is learned by association with other human beings, and without this tool we don't begin to be what we are capable of becoming.

Babies who are not given love and human touch often fail to live or are stunted in growth. Loneliness, the lack of human contact, can bring sickness and death, as James Lynch indicates in *The Broken Heart* (Basic, 1979).

The ordinary, healthy growth of the human soul requires this kind of human environment and then further human contact if the soul is to mature to its destiny. The person who is truly interested in soul growth will look for four different types of human relationship.

1. First of all the soul needs a religious institution. The idea that I can dig into the depths and discover by myself all I need to find out about religious reality is ridiculous. God and his world are *real* and have to be discovered. Any major religion is better than a private religious system. The People's Temple came to tragedy because the private religion of Jim Jones was taken as religious truth by a group of followers. Sharing in some traditional religion keeps one balanced and in touch with reality, keeps one from getting inflated, and is far less dangerous. *Beware of new religions.*

2. For modern educated Westerners, spiritual growth involves education and use of our critical capacities. We need a group in which issues can be brought up and discussed. The professor or computer programmer or lawyer who will not take the time and energy to study and learn about religious reality will not grow to full maturity. We all need a group of other learning and seeking individuals to keep us moving ahead.

3. Most spiritual seekers that I have known also need a group of other seekers to pray with and talk about the experiences which come to them when they are open. It is not easy to find such groups in most Christian churches. However, if we look sincerely one can find other people with

whom we can share and test the experiences we have had and have recorded in our journals. A group often begins with only two or three people.

4. A different kind of sharing usually takes place, however, when two people meet together again and again over a long period. A trust develops. This kind of situation can be one in which anything can be shared. Most human beings need at least one person with whom they can share on this level. Sometimes it is only as we read our journal writings to another that we hear them ourselves. Some writers on journals describe the practice of reading journal entries as voicing one's journal record. It is quite different to read one's writing out loud instead of letting another read it. Seldom do I know the full range of my feelings about what I have written until I read it to another.

Every Christian saint with whom I am acquainted has had a spiritual director, one with whom that person could share the totality of life. Often the spiritual state of the people with whom these spiritual giants shared was far inferior to that of the saints. However, sharing the full range of one's being with another keeps one humble and objective and keeps one's feet on the ground. This kind of sharing helps to keep one from getting exalted or inflated ideas about oneself or going off on a tangent. A journal is helpful in sharing with another. Unless one has recorded all of one's self, one's fears, angers, dreams (whatever they may be), lusts, ecstasies, and joys, one seldom is able to share all of one's self with another. I doubt if it is possible to present an objective view of one's self to another if one has not kept some written record of the depth of one's being.

5. If we are to listen to the depths of ourselves or to the inner beings who camp on the frontiers of our soul, we must

learn to listen to other human beings. Only as we have relationships with people who listen to us and to whom we listen can we develop that sensitivity which enables us to hear the many voices wishing to speak within us. When I learn to hear other people in their pain and anger and joy without judging them or their actions and without laying expectations on them, I learn to listen to myself and can then record a host of things which I might otherwise miss. The human soul-seed needs this kind of environment of love and cross-fertilization if it is to develop to its fullness.

Time, a record, and perseverance

Forcing growth on most living plants damages them and weakens them. Nothing is more necessary for the healthy growth of a plant than time. Growth takes time. There is no alternative. Time is a part of living things: seeds, plants, and animals, as well as souls.

I find that I need four quite different periods of time to allow my soul to send forth tender new shoots, leaves, and branches.

1. I need first of all the daily time which I have already described. This is my time for daily exposure of my total inner being to the light. How much I lose when I do not record these times of turning toward the center of love and meaning! This requires at least 20 to 40 minutes a day.

2. And then I need longer times once or twice a month or as often as I find something in my soul upsetting me or calling for attention and care. This is a time of special projects or periodic housecleaning for my inner soul room. I need to plan at least once a month to have two to three hours set aside for getting down to basics with myself, re-

flecting on how I am doing, establishing priorities, mapping out strategies for renewal, dealing with troublesome emotions, or expressing insights or joy in poetry, song, drawing, or story. This use of time is practically impossible without the practice of journal keeping. Seldom does one take that kind of time unless one has a journal to draw one aside to reflect. Good intentions for this kind of reflection are seldom realized except by those who have a habit of written reflection.

3. Once a year I need at least 36 to 48 hours to stop all my activity, take stock of where I am, and see if any major changes or reconstructions are indicated. If, indeed, one has a fruitful time of retreat and does not record the experience, often one does not actualize one's insights. Each year I enjoy going to the Benedictine monastery in Pecos, New Mexico, for such a time of inward retreat. It is like the dormant time that some plants need before a new time of growth. One of the great ministries of the Catholic Church is providing retreat centers where we human beings can get away and reflect. The finest single account of a time of inward reflection is still Anne Morrow Lindbergh's *Gift from the Sea* (Random, 1978).

4. And then I need little moments during the day to pause and ask quietly that God's presence may be with me so that I have something of value to say or do. Often in these brief minutes insights will come. Frank Laubach describes this practice in his pamphlet *The Game with Minutes.* Again the value of this quiet inward turning is likely to slip away like a wisp of cloud in the wind if I do not make some record of the more important flashes that come to me.

The tree leaves its natural record. When it dies or is cut down and one cuts at right angles to the trunk, the record of the tree's life is revealed. The rings of the tree are its living journal, written into its very fibre. These tree-ring records are so accurate that we can date pieces of wood found in charred posts and desert buildings to the very year in which the tree was cut down. The tree records all the major events of its life. It records its birth and death. All the great storms are shown in the rings, as are the droughts and the rainless and joyless years. And then there were the years when growth was full and rich. The rain and the sun were present along with gentle breezes.

Nature writes the record in the tree, but nature does not write the record in human beings. If men and women are to make records, they have to do it consciously. We are open to so many more influences than the tree. We are open to spiritual as well as to physical stimuli. We will never know the full import of our journey unless we make a conscious record. All of this information may be recorded in the unconscious, but it is only available to me as I make an outer record.

Human beings can change more than trees. They can uproot themselves, take themselves to new places, and direct their lives in new directions. A written record, a written reflection, can give us knowledge of where we are coming from and where we are going. Our very capacity to be changed and molded makes a journal an important instrument in a growing spiritual life.

Courage, persistence, and endurance of suffering are not very popular words in most modern vocabularies. In my study over my desk hangs an etching by George Elbert Burr entitled "Timberline Storm." It portrays a pine tree at the very edge of the timberline bearing the fury of a winter storm. Many of the branches have been destroyed by former storms. The tree is gnarled, but it is firm and solid, its roots sunk into the very rock. It has a wild beauty.

If I had made the universe I would have made it easier for human beings, but in making it easier I would undoubtedly have botched the whole affair. Many times I have called out in pain and anger, in doubt and despair, asking "Why? Why? Why?"

Many times Jesus spoke directly to the need for courage in the spiritual undertaking. He reminded us that the broad and easy way usually leads to anything but the kingdom of heaven. He spoke of a narrow gate and a steep path. He spoke of picking up one's cross and following him if we want to be his disciples.

The tree which survives must endure drought, storm, lightning, tempest, fire, and flood. One reason redwoods live so long is that their bark is fire resistant and they can endure the fires which sweep most forests at one time or another. No doubt some of this struggle is necessary for a tough and hardy tree or soul. But often trees are destroyed by storms and human souls are smashed like ships before a gale, becoming so much driftwood, lying and whitening on some forgotten beach.

The problem of evil is a very knotty one. It takes real discernment to decide which storms are for our good and which seem to come out of the angry pit of hell and evil. However, the important matter is how we respond to these storms. A journal can help us distinguish them. The storms for our growth can be integrated as we reflect on them. The evil storms can be sustained much more easily when we have another with us. When there is no other to whom we can talk, a journal gives companionship, support, and courage. When the storms are beating over me, it is helpful to have developed the ability to listen through the storm to a voice of concern on the other side. Imaginative recording of inner or outer storms also gives perspective and sinks roots deep into life.

The process of growth toward God is complex. A journal is not a substitute for the process, but a very helpful and creative part of it. In addition to a journal one needs a healthy soul and the capacity to have one's ordinary perceptions and ways of living cracked open. One also needs to know and describe a view of the universe which has a place for spiritual reality.

The unfolding plant needs light, and the soul needs the light of the God of love, the risen Christ, and the Holy Spirit. The human soul needs a community on the journey and the warmth of human caring which leads to divine caring.

How much we need patience to allow the growth to occur! We need time, time in which the various kinds of growth can take place. And last of all we need courage to hang on and find God and his blessings, as Jacob did when he wrestled at the brook of Jabbok. Paul Tillich clearly describes the necessity of this solid persistence in his excellent book, *The Courage to Be* (Yale, 1952).

One can lose one's way on this inner journey. We want to be sure that the bogs and cliffs on the journey are well marked. They are part of the journey, and so we need to look at them next.

6

The Dangers
of Journal Keeping

T HE ONLY WAY to avoid all danger is to cease to live. We are in danger whenever we set out on the highway in our car. We are in danger of betrayal whenever we make a friend. Even in the fortress of our own home we may be set upon and attacked. In the forests there are wild beasts and in the cities there are savage human beings. There are quicksands, crumbling cliffs, falling trees, and killer waves. I am not suggesting that we seek out a tropical island to avoid danger, but rather that we face, acknowledge, and deal with the inevitable dangers so we can live as safely and creatively as possible.

In pointing out the dangers of the inner journey which a journal can stimulate and record, I am not suggesting that most people avoid the journey. I am simply pointing out the pitfalls so that the journey can be as fruitful and meaningful as possible. On the whole we children of Western civilization are far better acquainted with the outer physical dangers than we are with those of the spiritual or psychic world. It is difficult to examine carefully what one believes does not exist.

If one is going to deal with the inner world, it is infinitely safer to record one's journey in writing than to go at it blind, without a record. One of the greatest helps in dealing with the spiritual world is keeping a record, but once one begins to write there are certain dangers specifically related to journal keeping.

Automatic writing

Looking back over your journal, you will notice that the writing in your record is noticeably different when you are possessed with different moods. Sometimes in moments of clarity you will turn to printing, without realizing that you have changed your form of writing. In bursts of anger your handwriting will be quite different from those times when you are expressing love and joy. Handwriting is so much a part of our personalities that it can reveal our very character. Some European universities offer degrees in handwriting analysis. Over the years I have changed, and my handwriting has changed also.

When I begin to write in quietness, it is possible that something quite unlike my ordinary personality may begin to be expressed. Thoughts, attitudes, and insights sometimes begin to flow effortlessly. Often at such times my handwriting changes markedly. It is as if my hands were possessed by some reality other than my conscious personality. The language is far different than what I ordinarily use. Sometimes it is as if something or someone other than myself were trying to speak to me or through me.

Few Westerners have any knowledge of this kind of phenomena, and such an experience often gives a sense of excitement and fascination. It is very easy when one has such experiences to become inflated and think that one has a pipe-line to some new source of wisdom and power. One can become possessed by a psychic reality which may be a part of one's psyche or be outside one's being. The inner voices which speak in this way are often seductive and try to convince individuals that they are above human scrutiny.

One needs to subject all such writings to deep and careful discernment. I have described the process of evaluating these autonomous voices from within in my book *Discernment, A Study in Ecstasy and Evil* (Paulist, 1978). It is enough at this juncture to point out that the divine and the angelic seldom wish to possess human beings, while the neutral or demonic are much more likely to wish to use and take over one's psyche.

Automatic writing can be encouraged through the use of a planchette. A piece of wood with casters to permit easy movement is fitted with a pencil or pen to write on the paper underneath. The hand is placed lightly on the planchette. Often writing occurs which is quite different from that which is characteristic of the person using it. The Ouija board is similar, but in the latter the letters are printed on the supporting board and a pointer spells out the message. Automatic writing, use of an Ouija board, mediumship (where the individual apparently allows a spirit guide to take over the personality), and prophecy all share the same dangers. It is difficult to know the source of the material. Is it coming from an unconscious part of the psyche or from outside the psyche? When it does seem to come from outside one's own personality, it is necessary to discern whether the message is coming from the divine, from some destructive psychic content, or from some lost, misguided, and unembodied human soul. It is wise to remember that any secondary good which pretends to be the greatest good carries the very essence of evil.

Abandoning one's self to whatever spirit wishes to take over and control one is very dangerous business. It is my firm belief that human beings are meant to be encountered and not possessed. For this reason I look with real doubt on the use of hypnotism for purposes other than the relief of pain where no other palliative is available. Seeking any of these experiences is very dangerous. When these things occur autonomously, they should be dealt with carefully and critically. Some Christian groups are afraid of journal keeping because they believe it necessarily leads to automatic writing. As a matter of fact, automatic writing is a relatively rare occurrence.

A minister wrote to me because he was worried about automatic writing among some members of his congregation. He had introduced the idea of meditation to a small group. One person in the group found that she had the gift of automatic writing. She also became convinced that she was a special mouthpiece of the spirit world. The minister knew the woman well and believed that this interest in the spirit world was more likely a compensation for a very unhappy marriage. The parishioner would accept no evaluation of her experience, and she led some others to a kind of spiritualistic religion.

Inflation and retreat from the world

When one's journal writing leads to an inflated opinion of one's connection with spiritual reality it can also be quite dangerous. One of the tests of prophecy is the kind of person who prophesies. The validity of an insight can usually be tested by how it is integrated into the life of the one who had it. The idea that one has special value because one has insights can lead to real trouble. Most often when ordinary people think they have a special connection with divine reality, they are inflated and not very critical. Any special insight should be checked out with the critical evaluation of another so that one does not get into nonsense. I am suspicious of those who feel themselves above this kind of critical evaluation.

If one's insight is quite different from the religious tradition in which one was reared, there is double reason for caution. Self-interest and self-aggrandizement can motivate journal writing. This is why it is so wise to have some group or individual who can give an objective response to what has been written. One can be in touch with many psychic realities other than God and his host of angels.

Whenever one's record of the inner life takes the place of human relationships, one is in danger. If the center of reality is love, then in addition to coming into relationship with this reality one needs to develop loving relations with other human beings. Kierkegaard's lack of real contact with other human beings casts doubts on the genuineness of his deep inner experience and the thousands of pages which he wrote. Nietzsche had deep contact with inner reality, but no close human friend. Our journal writing should make us more outgoing, loving, and relatable, or else something has gone wrong. A journal is no substitute for living.

Introverts will find it easier to keep a journal, but harder to step out into the world and implement their insights. They need that balance. Extraverts need times of withdrawal and reflection to keep a balance. It is an introvert for whom a journal can be a substitute for living, seldom an extravert.

In many Eastern religions the physical world is viewed as illusory. Religious persons are expected to be detached from physical reality and ordinary living. However, one pays one's due to society and the outer world. Within such a tradition it is possible to view the inner spiritual world and one's dealings with it in one's writings as more important than the outer physical world. When a Westerner takes the stance that the inner world is more significant and important than dealing with outer reality, that person is often in real danger. One of my former students described such a trip to the East which resulted in a state of near disorientation.

One can become so involved in the inner world that one loses contact with the outer one. Inability to deal with ordinary reality is mental illness. Some people are so close to the inner world that they should be encouraged away from journal keeping and out into relationships with people and things. One person's meat can be another's poison. Journal keeping can be dangerous when it becomes an escape from living rather than a place of reflection which leads to more adequate living.

Other dangers

One form of escapist journal keeping is going over and over the same problem and never acting on the insights one has obtained. Writing down solutions and solving real problems are quite different activities. A journal should be a goad to inner and outer action.

Some people are very close to the unconscious. They can become intoxicated by the beauty of images and stories which rise out of the depths of the psyche and beyond. Thus they fail to see that the writings which pour out of them are more than poetry. Such writings usually direct individuals toward some goal. Seeing journal writing as only art can rob it of its transforming value.

When the keeping of a journal leads one into depression, something is wrong. Some people live on the edge of an abyss. When writing in one's journal drags one deeper into fear and depression, something is amiss and one should probably continue only with expert counsel and advice. There are some levels of darkness which one should not try to penetrate. There are some abysses which we should avoid at all costs.

A psychiatrist sent me a woman on the verge of psychotic depression. As we talked I discovered that she thought she had to encounter and get to the bottom of every darkness that came her way. The darkness was more than she could handle. It was swallowing her up. She learned to put Christ between her and that darkness, and she has become stabilized and avoided a breakdown. One does not need to be heroic. The purpose of Christ's death and resurrection was to defeat evil and give us power over it through him. We don't have to take it on ourselves. When we think we must or can, we have once more fallen into inflation.

Sometimes we are depressed because of outer tragedy or conflict. When this is the case it is foolish to look for inner causes. A journal can simply help us weight outer problems with inner darknesses. Sometimes following flu or other sickness there is a physical cause for depression. Again, it is not worthwhile looking for inner causes for such darkness.

It is also dangerous to start on the inner journey simply to keep a journal, because it is difficult to stop once one has begun. Once one is opened to a new level of consciousness, there is no way I know of by which one can go back and become unconscious again. A journal can open us to a whole new realm and level of reality which then makes its claims on us. If we try to withdraw we can get into trouble. Journal keeping can be addictive. Once we have found a reality in the inner world through a journal, we are seldom totally satisfied with the outer one again. Again it should be stressed that *dealing with the depth of the inner world is not for everyone,* but rather for those who find that they are called to it.

Some people are thrown into the unconscious, and they must deal with it. For them journal keeping is simply a means of survival and of dealing with the unconscious. Others may be deeply drawn to the inner way and find they have to deal with that reality. Again, a journal is for them a virtual necessity. It can be a doorway into a new level of reality. No one should enter without caution and care. If any of the above dangers occur, one should terminate the use of a journal and seek the advice of a spiritual director who has entered the territory, survived, and flourished.

Avoiding danger

One great value of a written record is the fact that it is there in black and white. One can return to it and reread what has been written with critical objectivity, as if it were written by someone else. One danger of prophetic utterance is that it is spoken and shared before one can evaluate the message. What pours out of us as we write need not be acted on or shared with others.

One can avoid the dangers I have described by carefully

rereading what comes through one and sharing with someone who is wise in this area before one takes anything as
divine truth. As we read through what we have written we
can see how this fits in with our basic view of the world
and how it corresponds with other historical religions.

Many people have experiences of being in another time as
another person. Sometimes this other person speaks through
the pages of a journal. Often these people jump to the idea
of reincarnation. Because they do not use their critical capacities, they fail to see that a theory of the collective unconscious
can make such an experience possible without all that goes
with the idea of reincarnation. They may have touched a
psychic reality in the deep unconscious, but this does not
mean they have been that person.

In journal keeping, as elsewhere in real religion, a critical,
careful, questioning spirit is necessary if one is not to be
subject to superstition and nonsense. Without this critical,
evaluative ability, even religious experience can lead us
astray. Von Hügel has pointed out again and again that
critical objectivity is one of the essential elements of mature
religion.

Another element which von Hügel stresses as essential to
genuine religious life is a historical religion. Those who
think that they can come up with a full religious view
from their own inner experience are inflated. We need our
historical roots as much in religion as elsewhere. Our journal
insights should be checked against the religious tradition
which we know best.

Often our insights will reveal to us parts of that tradition
which we had overlooked or failed to understand. Our insights are confirmed when we find them in a part of the
tradition we had not understood before. Likewise the depth

and validity of the religious tradition is verified. An amazing aspect of the New Testament is its depth. As I have spent more and more time with the one who speaks within, I come to see more meaning and depth in the sayings and actions of Jesus of Nazareth. When my journal experience confirms and deepens my understanding of my religious tradition, it is safest and most likely to be healthy.

I have found it helpful over the years to have a group of people with whom I could share my inner experiences. Some insights which I did not see as valuable were valuable to some in the group. Sometimes the group questioned some of what I brought. For 20 years my inner listening and the recording of it in my journal was the source of most of my sermons. When one of these sermons struck a chord in the congregation, I knew that I had struck deep in my inner encounter. I have also learned much from others who shared in prayer groups. Every church should try to provide a place where those who are on the inner way and keeping journals can meet and share their encounters, failures, fears, and ecstasies. When the church does not provide such groups people are forced to find community outside of its wisdom and restraint.

There are some things within me which are so personal that I can only share these in private with one whom I totally trust. I have had many friends with whom I have shared throughout the years. I believe that my spiritual life and my journal writing would have come to a standstill had it not been for those friends who listened with wisdom, sometimes warning me and sometimes encouraging me. There is no greater need in the church today than for men and women trained as spiritual guides. We need the friendship and guidance of those who have lived deeply in the inner world and will share our journey with us. Every church worthy of its name will try to provide this kind of one-to-one spiritual communion.

There are great religious experiences which seem to defy any attempt to express them. Some people have a sense of union with the divine which meets all needs and longings. These experiences are of great value. However, we humans do not stay in this condition long, as St. Teresa of Avila reminds us, and we also need to keep journals with words and images to help us grow in the spiritual way. It is even helpful to try to describe the great experiences in poetry, as St. John of the Cross did in his great religious poetry. These experiences can also be expressed in painting, music, dance, or any other art form. When we think we have attained such a state of contemplation that we no longer need to record dreams, conversations, and images, we have most likely fallen into inflation.

The discipline of daily journal keeping can help one avoid getting inflated or taking oneself too seriously. As one turns inward day after day and records what comes, one realizes how often one is dry, how often one is motivated by selfish-ness and anger and not by love, how far one is from total union with God. When we know all of ourselves, we have little temptation to see ourselves as perfect and we need no hair shirts to make us humble.

7

Seventeen Suggestions
for Interpreting
Your Dreams

In coming to know God I have found two practices which have helped me more than any others. The first has been the nightly dialog with God which I have recorded in my journal and which I have already discussed in an earlier chapter. The other has been listening to my dreams and realizing that a wisdom greater than mine wished to communicate with me.

In the process of dialoging, once I realized God was waiting for me, it was I who made the first initiative. In the dreams it was the other who made the first effort at communication with me. The message came again and again, whether I understood it or not. The other never lost patience. If indeed the dream message came from God, this continuous knocking at the doorway of my soul speaks eloquently of the incredible providence of God, his continual caring. He is indeed the prodigal Father, the Christ reaching out to us before we ever thought of turning to him.

I have discovered no better way to convince agnostic college students that they are not alone than encouraging them to keep a record of their dreams. After six months of recording dreams most of them have been convinced that some wisdom greater than their own has been trying to break through to them. They also began to wonder who this "dreamer within" was. Who was the one who knew all about them, spoke unerringly about the places where they had gone off the track, knew the way back onto the path of meaning and hope, and even gave directions on how to get back on the right track? Occasionally they had dreams of numinous or holy power.

The study of dream symbolism is vast and complicated. Volumes have been written on the subject. In the study of physics, there are two levels. The first is theoretical, which has little or no immediate application. Then there is applied physics, which helps us light our houses and manage our plumbing. The theoretical study is necessary if there is going to be practical use of that knowledge. However, one need know very little physics to keep the drains flowing and the fuses changed. There is the same kind of difference in understanding one's dreams. The theoretical studies of dreams are very important and valuable, but all I wish to give at this juncture are some practical methods of trying to hear the essential messages of dreams.

Many people will want to know more about interpreting dreams than I can provide in a manual on journal keeping. I have written a simple little book, *Dreams, A Way to Listen to God* (Paulist, 1978), which is written for the person who finds the idea of dreams as divine messages totally new, and in it an annotated bibliography is included. John Sanford has written a more thorough study of dreams in his recent book, *Dreams and Healing* (Paulist, 1979). A student of Mr. Sanford's has written a practical and helpful book which gives many useful illustrations of how to understand one's dreams within the Christian framework; it is *Digging Deep* by Robert L. Schwenck (Dove, 1979). My book, *God, Dreams, and Revelation* (Augsburg, 1974), shows that there was a significant interest in dreams in the Bible and the early church.

How I began to listen to dreams

Sometime in 1949 I began to keep a journal. I am not sure why I began. I took my prayer life more seriously. Insights began to come and I started to record them. About this time I read one of Fritz Kunkel's books. He emphasized the importance of dreams. When an important or moving dream occurred, it seemed natural to record it in my journal.

Nothing in my childhood, college, or seminary training had ever pointed to dreams as important. Indeed, I had been thoroughly indoctrinated by a rationalistic and materialistic view of the world. It seemed perfectly ridiculous to think that something of importance could come out of anything so irrational as dreams. As I started to spend more time in prayer and journal keeping this superior attitude toward communication with God gradually eroded away.

In May of 1951 I came to a dead-end street. As I look back on the months before this time I can see that my dreams were warning me of dangers ahead. I remember one dream of trying to take up the offering through the branches of a dead tree which had fallen through the church building. I awoke in terror! My wife and children were forced through an illness in the family to spend nearly two months 3000 miles away. I was left alone in California, and at that time the inner confusion really broke forth.

Jung has stated that most neuroses in people over age 35

are the result of being cut off from contact with that reality of which all the great religions of humankind speak. I was indeed cut off from an experiential knowledge of this reality. As I got up in the pulpit to preach, a voice speaking from my left shoulder would whisper: "But you don't believe any of that claptrap." Ministers who are trying to provide meaning for others are in a doubly bad place when they find they have no direct knowledge to impart. Neuroses in rationalistic clergy may well be a tribute to their essential integrity. Seminaries provide inferred knowledge of God and not direct or immediate knowledge of the other.

I went to see a friend, Dorothy Phillips, who was the co-author of a fine book, *The Choice Is Always Ours* (Theosophical Publ., 1975). She was a part of my parish in Monrovia, California. She spoke of her analyst and dream interpretation in the same way some women discuss their favorite market. She directed me to Dr. Max Zeller, whom I have already mentioned. With his help I began to understand the messages coming through the dreams. With this help my inner confusion became less oppressive. Even more important, I came to know the dreamer within who had been sending me messages which I had ignored and not understood. Within a short time my life had a new depth and direction, and I had new assurance of God's reality. When my wife returned in two months she hardly knew the man who welcomed her home. During the years which have followed I have learned that a wisdom and love speaks through dreams, a voice which seeks to guide me and bring the totality of me to reality itself.

I have learned that my dreams speak to me as an individual. They are tailored to me as a "well-made suit," to use John Sanford's phrase. At the same time dreams use symbols, language, and stories which may often have universal human meaning. Dreams have many levels of meaning. For most modern Westerners they speak a language which is unintelligible. It is, however, a language which can be learned and which children and primitives understand more easily than the products of most Western educational systems.

Sometimes dreams speak with a clarity which can scarcely be missed, but most often they speak in the language of pictures, symbols, fairy tales, and myths. One has to work in order to understand their meaning. God gives us dreams to help us manage our lives and bring us to the other. He does not do the managing himself, as some religious enthusiasts fail to understand. Dreams give us clues as to how to run our lives, but they require our cooperation and work. Learning to listen to dreams may well be learning to listen and work *actively* with God.

Seventeen suggestions

At a recent conference of Christians wishing to understand more about dreams I was asked to summarize as simply as possible how ordinary people could understand them. These were the suggestions that came to me as I answered that question:

1. The person who has already purchased a journal and a pencil to go with it has already responded to the first suggestion. If one is to keep a record of dreams, one has to have a notebook at one's bedside and be ready to spend a few moments reflecting on the events of the night as one wakes up. Most dreams are lost forever if we do not record them within five minutes of awakening. Dreams can be lost if we are wandering around looking for a pad and pencil. The

radio alarm clock also brings one out of sleep with attention riveted on the outer world, and thus also ruins much dream recall. Most people need seven hours sleep if they are to recall a significant number of dreams. The best dreams often come after seven hours of sleep. Dreams must be valued and seen as important if they are to be recalled. Dreams have to be remembered before they can be interpreted, as the book of Daniel reminds us.

2. The next step in understanding dreams is to write them down. This preserves them from oblivion, and the very act of writing them down sometimes unlocks their meaning. It also fixes dreams before one so they can be returned to again and again. They should be written down simply. If the recording of an ordinary dream takes more than ten minutes, something is wrong.

Without these first two steps there is little or no dream interpretation in our society and culture. In some societies dreams are discussed along with breakfast. When dreams are treated in this way, written records are not as essential as among us Westerners.

3. As one writes down a dream the first question to ask is, What is this dream trying to say to me? Then one can ask, What general impression does the dream make on me? Is it happy or sad, filled with emotion or detached? What is it trying to convey?

4. Sometimes this first attempt at understanding draws a blank. Then one can go back to the dream after some time has elapsed and imagine it is the dream of a friend one knows well. One reason why dreams are difficult to understand is that they come from the unconscious. Therefore their meaning is foreign to us. Sometimes a dream will reveal its meaning when we look at it as a production in

no way related to us, as something totally outside of us. In other words, we pretend it is someone else's dream.

5. Once one gets into this frame of reference one can imagine that a dream is a play or a movie which one has seen or a picture which has caught one's attention in a magazine or at an art gallery. What message would the movie be giving if the dream were a movie? What would the photographer or artist have been trying to convey if the dream were such a picture?

6. Alan McGlashan speaks of the "dreamer within" who gives us the dream. Imagine that you are talking to the one who has put on the dream production. Ask the dreamer within what he or she is trying to tell you with the dream. What is the message? In order to have success in this process, one must first quiet down and be still. I have suggested how this can be done in Chapter 3.

7. After hearing me give one lecture on dreams, one person became convinced that dreaming was a way God could speak to her. She did not think that she ordinarily dreamed, but found that as soon as she expectantly put a pad and pencil by her bed she could remember her dreams. Her first dream was a powerful one which changed her life. She interpreted it as far as she could and then brought it into the church before the reserved sacrament. She prayed for understanding, and understanding was given. The dream was telling her about her daughter who had been depressed and how to help her toward health. When understood in prayer the dream gave her hope in her daughter's recovery and then helped her facilitate the healing process.

As she continued to bring the dream before God in prayerful asking and listening, she realized that it also spoke of the sickness of her own inner "child" who had been imprisoned and unloved. The dream gave her many months of material to work on in prayer (see my book *Dreams, A Way to Listen to God*, pp. 55ff.). Those who have found real meaning and answers in prayer will often find meaning in their dreams by bringing them before God with a prayerful attitude. When Joseph was asked in Egypt who there was who could interpret dreams, he replied, "Do not interpretations belong to God?" (Gen. 40:8). This woman found that God has not changed. He will still help us to understand our dreams when we ask him.

8. One can then look at the individual dream symbols and ask, Do the symbols have any particular or significant meaning? There are volumes written on some dream symbols. Sometimes it helps to look up the meaning of symbols which leave one completely in the dark. J. E. Cirlot has provided us with *A Dictionary of Symbols* (Philosophical Library, 1972). It can be helpful if one uses the suggestions *only* as suggestions. In the indices of the *Collected Works* (Princeton) and of *The Visions Seminars* (Spring Publications, 1976) of C. G. Jung one can find many helpful explanations of the meaning of many symbols. *It is of great importance to remember that one's personal associations with dreams take precedence over the meanings provided by another person or found in any book.* We need to remember that only when the meaning of a symbol or dream "clicks" with the individual who dreamed it is it correct.

9. Sometimes one can dialog with one's dream symbols and ask them who they are or what they mean. When a symbol recurs again and again, it is usually telling us that we have not yet understood the message of the dream. It is surprising what insights come when we dialog with a dream symbol like a gorilla, turtle, rug, or a tree. It is almost as if

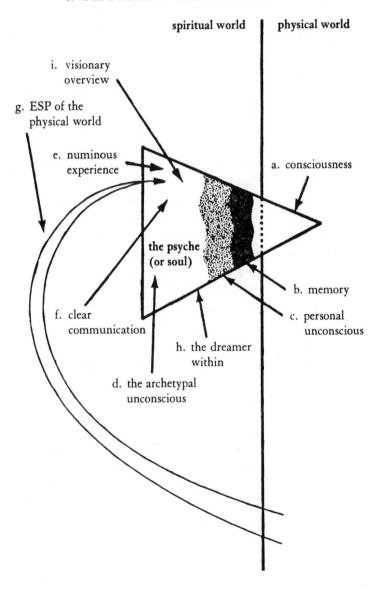

the dream symbol is just waiting to be asked its meaning so it can reveal itself.

10. It is important to realize that when we dream of other people, the meaning is usually not about them, but about a part of ourselves which is like that person. Most dreams are telling us about ourselves, the various parts of ourselves, and how we can be brought to wholeness and healing. Most dreams do not tell us about other people or outer events.

11. This brings us to the point of realizing that dreams can refer to many different areas of our inner lives. It is helpful to see which area a dream is pointing to. The diagram on p. 113 gives us a picture of the various areas to which a dream can refer. In this diagram the right side represents the physical world and our ordinary conscious perception of it. The left side represents the nonphysical world and the depths of the soul.

It is valuable to discern which part of the psyche and the spiritual world is being expressed in a dream. What part of me is speaking most clearly? All nine levels may be present in a dream, but one needs to decide which one is presenting the dominant message. Most people find these nine levels within them from time to time, although some are far more rare than others.

a. Sometimes a dream refers mainly to yesterday's events and their significance, but seldom without some alteration in the scene. One can always ask one's self why this particular event from a former day has been seized upon and highlighted by the dreamer within. In 30 years of listening to my own dreams and 25 of listening to others' dreams, I have found that dreams which merely repeat yesterday's events are really quite rare, in spite of the old wives' tale to the contrary.

b. A dream can reproduce anything from memory, even a scene quite inaccessible to conscious recall, for instance a scene from second grade in school, in full color with names and faces. Nothing in one's life seems to be lost beyond remembrance to the dreamer within.

c. Sometimes a dream brings forth actions and thoughts of the past which we have repressed and forgotten because they cause us pain. The personal unconscious is not locked to the dreamer within. This kind of dream can bring up important material.

d. One of the great discoveries of both Freud and Jung was that there are universal symbols which bubble up out of the soul and tell us of its very nature and structure. This area of the soul has been named the "collective unconscious" by Jung. Understanding this level requires much study and application.

e. Some dreams are charged with numinous or awe-inspiring power. When something beyond our soul touches us and is known, there is usually a sense of awe and holy fear. This can bring terror if it is some evil or demonic reality, amazement if it is some deceased person or an angelic or neutral spiritual reality, or ecstasy if God is the one who touches our soul. We call such visions of the night "numinous dreams."

f. Sometimes the message of a dream comes through clearly in a direct and understandable sentence or two. I have argued with God that he should speak like this more often. The answer which has come to me is that God is more interested in his relationship with me than in giving me information. When I puzzle over a dream I spend more time with him.

g. Dreams are the natural altered state of consciousness,

and *very occasionally* we are given knowledge in dreams of the physical world which we do not get through ordinary sensory channels. This information can cross space and time, and even tell of the future. *One of the most dangerous uses of dreams is to expect that they are always or usually speaking of the future.* Only one or two percent of dreams have this meaning, and no one can tell which ones foretell the future until after an event has occurred. Most superstitious and silly uses of dreams involve using them for fortune telling. But occasionally they do give this kind of information.

h. From some deep center of reality the dreamer within speaks. He or she knows everything about us, has a wisdom greater than ours, and provides these nightly dramas for our transformation. I believe this dreamer within is none other than the Holy Spirit which God gives as our inner guide, friend, and comforter.

i. Once or twice in a life, often near the end of it, we human beings are given a glimpse of life beyond us, a visionary overview of reality, of the divine center of love at the core of existence. These, of course, are the great revelatory experiences for which we all hope. They seldom come or are appreciated, however, unless we have been working on and listening to our dreams.

12. Sometimes when one has not been able to find any insight about a dream one can read it out loud to a friend. Often hearing a dream read unlocks its meaning. Sometimes when I read one to my friend John Sanford, the dream reveals itself before he says a word in response. It is important to have a friend who is attuned to spiritual things and can at least take the idea of dreams and dream interpretation seriously.

13. Not everyone can find a person skilled in dream analy-

sis. If, however, one prays for someone with whom one can discuss the reality of the spiritual world and one's dreams, God's hand will not be foreshortened. He can still give direction in finding someone to help. Jung once said that we receive the analyst we deserve!

We can ask these other people what they see in a dream. Sometimes they can show us something which was obvious but which we were blind to because we were so close to the dream. Remember, however, that no dream interpretation is to be taken seriously unless it fits, unless it clicks with meaning and relevance to the dreamer. Some people find a group helpful in which dreams are discussed as a part of a larger program.

If one is in deep trouble, then it is important to find some professional to whom one can turn. Again, God will direct individuals to help. Whenever we think our souls are not worth the trouble of travel and money, we devalue the one who found us of enough value that he would have died for us even if we had been the only one. One must usually pay for professional help, and sometimes the fact we do pay can be of help to us. We take it more seriously.

14. One can also use the imagination in other ways than simply dialoging with the dream symbols or the dreamer within. This requires some knowledge of imagination in prayer such as I have outlined in *The Other Side of Silence*. Here are some suggestions of how this can be done.

a. We can go back into the dream in our waking imagination and allow a dream which was not completed to complete itself. Often this will give us great insight.

b. We can also return to a negative, painful, and destructive dream and imagine that, with Christ at one's side, instead of coming out to the original tragic or destructive conclusion, it came out to quite another one. Sometimes reversing a negative dream can actually change the destructive aspects of one's inner life which led to the dream. Dr. Rosalind Cartwright, a University of Illinois psychology professor, has advocated just such a method of reshaping one's dreams in order to give relief to suffering patients.

c. In a dream which leaves one puzzled or frightened one can return into it with Christ as one's companion. He can show us its meaning and bring it to a better conclusion. The one who conquered death and evil can handle any situation which a dream presents. We shall give an example of this creative imagining in the next section of this chapter.

15. When one has finished one's work with a dream, it is very helpful to write down what the dream has meant in a paragraph or two. This concludes the process of working on a dream and also sometimes adds some final insights about the dream and one's life.

16. *Dreams are not good or bad in themselves.* "Good" dreams show one the potentiality which lies ahead and into which one can step if one wishes to. "Bad" dreams show what needs to be avoided in one's life. Being as lazy as most of us are, bad dreams often have a more positive effect on us than good dreams, because they frighten us into action.

17. It is important to *actualize* the dream situation. When I have a dream of a car running backwards and being unable to control it, it is necessary that I first stop and see in what way I am going backwards and out of control. Then I must *take steps to change that situation in my life.* When I dream of a snakebite in which my life is deeply touched by the deep unconscious, it tells me that there is positive potential ahead, but unless I get up early and work at my writing that potential cannot be realized. When a great experience is

given in a dream, it is our natural inclination to simply bask in it. One should at least write poetry or a story about the experience. Perhaps this will lead one to see what aspect of one's life needs to be emphasized and given freedom, so that the positive experience can be fulfilled.

Most people in most places have viewed dreams as divine gifts to give understanding and direction to life both here and into eternity. Jung has suggested that only the group of people who inhabit that peninsula of Asia known as Europe and their descendants have lost touch with the spiritual world to which dreams give access. They have also ignored dreams themselves, which are still a means of gaining access to that world.

Creative imagination transforming a dream

A long-time friend of ours has been working on her dreams for nearly a decade. She is a creative artist with great potential in many areas. She is married and has one child. Her actual situation is a very happy one—a fine and loving husband, a capable child, and many accomplishments to her credit—yet she has a difficult time seeing her own self-worth. This devaluation springs from her parents. They are unconscious souls who are part of a religious sect which allows salvation only for those in the sect. Others are damned. My friend has broken from the sect and is trying to establish her own identity and value.

In February of this year she had the following dream:

I was with a group of women; it was some type of party but very boring to me. I decided to leave early, but before going I noticed a small baby lying on a couch. The poor child looked as if it hadn't been fed recently.

I decided to breast-feed the child, knowing full well that I wouldn't have any milk. Well, to my surprise, the milk began to flow. The baby became very cheerful, laughing and happy.

The mother came; she looked like an irresponsible young thing. I thought that she was going to take the baby and go home, but she preferred to party. And in leaving, she told me that the baby was retarded anyway.

My friend realized that this dream spoke of her own vision of herself. It portrayed her inner idiot. A few days later she wrote the following fantasy, which lifted her mood and gave her a real sense of value once again. Seldom have I seen a better example of the process of turning a dream around in imaginative prayer.

I am sitting and cursing myself for being such a fool! "I am nothing," I tell myself. "Unintelligent, worthless—an idiot!" How I hate myself. Who would ever want and care for me?

The more I tell myself these things, of course, the gloomier I get. The world is horrible! No redemption, happiness, nothing!

The time passes, and I feel there's no hope. Hopelessness completely takes over. I am temporarily shaken from this mood, for a knock comes on the door—I open it, and there before me stands a most hideous-looking hag! She is holding a bundle. The bundle is, of course, a baby.

She tells me to take care of it for awhile. "No one will," she said. She had been door-to-door, but each person had refused her.

The hag told me just to care for the child awhile.

Well, certainly I thought of refusing. I don't have time to care for any baby. And what right does the ugly creature standing in front of me have to tell me to take care of a brat!

The hag's eyes looked as if they were reaching to my very soul. I began to tremble. "Well," I said, "Don't be too long." She said, "I won't be long, and I thank you." She handed me the baby and left.

It scarcely weighed anything, and I thought maybe the woman had fooled me and handed me nothing but blankets.

I began to take the blankets away from the child. I gave a scream of fright, for I was holding a most deformed-looking child. It was the most hideous of idiots. I put the child down and ran away from it! "What has this woman done to me?" I dared not enter into that room again.

After awhile, the child began to whimper. It was probably hungry, but I dared not feed it, let alone touch it. What was I to do?

The child then began to cry. A pathetic, desperate cry of complete helplessness. No one wanted it, no one loved or cared for it. One would rather have it rot than touch it.

The crying increased! What was I to do? I began wringing my hands in desperation. The child needed help, and I was the one left to do it.

I went into the room to the child. I looked into its face. How revolting! How horrible! I picked the baby up, and it quit crying. I could barely look into its face.

I had no bottle with which to feed it; it was too young to drink from a cup. What was I to do? My breasts began to throb. They felt hardened and full, as the breasts of a woman who nurses her child.

My blouse became soaked with milk that was pouring out of my breasts. How could this be? I have no baby myself.

I put the idiot to my breasts and he eagerly began drinking from my life. I looked down at the deformed head and little body, its twisted arms and legs. The color of its skin was not even normal.

"How pathetic," I said. "No one to care for the wretched creature. No one to love it."

I began stroking its head and arms. Its claw-like hand grabbed one of my fingers. It had finally found someone.

I began to cry! Tears of compassion; tears of hope; tears of joy; tears of love; tears for this baby. I had reached out and touched someone who needed love. I quickly forgot my own helplessness, uselessness. I was looking down into the face of my own inner idiot who until this time I dared not look at and recognize—this inner idiot who needs love, nourishment, and care. If I don't care for this idiot, I will be thrown into despair and inner death.

My tears washed the child's head. He turned from my breast and looked into my face and smiled and laughed. His face no longer looked ugly and frightening. I was looking into the face of the Christ Child. The Christ Child in me.

I turned and looked at the open door. There standing in the doorway was a beautiful woman. She told me that she had come to take the child, and appreciated what I had done for this little one. I realized that this beautiful woman was the hag that first brought me the Child.

8

Journaling
in Depth

IF I AM TO BRING all of me to the divine lover for renewal
and transformation, I need to look at all of me and face all
of me. Jung has remarked that one of the most difficult tasks
which faces any of us is to accept ourselves, a task which is
nearly impossible to fulfill. The example with which we
concluded the last chapter shows that this kind of work
takes time. This kind of imaginative effort requires more
than half an hour hewed out of a busy day. It requires a
period of several hours every two or three weeks in which
one can be still, turn inward, and allow the creative depths
within one to work in bringing transformation.

Few modern people do this kind of work, for it is most
demanding labor. One has to set a time aside for it if one is
going to get at it. As I have already mentioned, I find that
I need periods of several hours in length once every two or
three weeks for such inward turning. There are times of
crisis and tension when I need this kind of time more often.
Also, once a year I need a period of 36 to 48 hours to quiet
down, take a fresh look at my life, and listen to the deepest
voices speaking within me and hear what they have to say.

Anne Morrow Lindbergh's *Gift from the Sea* is the result
of such a creative time alone.

I have already suggested that one excellent way to begin
is to write out one's reasons for keeping a journal and sketch
out one's view of the world and the place of human beings
in it. In these two chapters I will outline eight different
ways in which a journal may be used in depth. These are
open-ended suggestions which can keep one at journal keeping as long as one's hand can hold a pencil or punch a typewriter key. I will give examples of each of these as I go
along. These examples are meant to inspire your own processes in your own individual way.

Reflecting consciously

At times of inner quandary or confusion, there are few
things which help more than stopping and going into a
quiet place, pencil in hand, to sort out the pressures, fears,
angers, and tensions which seem to be overwhelming me.
The very process of stopping begins to give me some control
over my life once again. I am able to describe just how I
feel and why. I can list, one by one, the things which are
bothering me. It is strange how much less oppressive they
seem when they are listed out in front of me in black and
white. Then as I read them over I can see which of these
things needs to be dealt with and which are only fearful
shadows which can be dismissed.

Usually I find that as I face the things before me I can
deal with each of them and can bear the worst that they
can bring. When I get to that point I am no longer para-
lyzed by panic and can begin to deal creatively with what
needs to be done. Known fears are nearly always easier to

deal with than unknown ones. Floating anxiety is difficult to bear just because one cannot put one's finger on it.

One of the best examples of this kind of reflection came to me recently from a friend and former student. We had been through a great deal together. During his senior year in college I was on a year's leave of absence and he slipped back to old attitudes and away from his journal keeping. I replied to a letter of desperation and he then wrote the following letter, which contained an entry from his journal.

Dear Morton,

. . . Your last letter to me in the midst of my depression chased the clouds away, so to speak. I must admit that it took quite a few readings of it before it began to sink to my depths, and as it did I felt you reaching out with your love. It was profound and beautiful.

As I look back on it, your words to me marked a turning point. Back from "the East," I feel more comfortable with myself than I have before. As John Donne would say, I feel closer to "the path of my heart's desire." Surely, there are still many "kinks" to be worked out, but I feel that I'm on firmer ground now. When you said "when it hurts too much you run and hide from yourself, but not for long . . ." I didn't know what you meant. After I let it sink in I could really feel what you meant and knew it to be very true. I've started writing again in my journal and perhaps the best indication of how I'm doing is to share with you some excerpts. (That way I won't have to struggle so much for words!)

"It feels good to once again pick up this journal, setting aside some time to be with myself and to do some reflecting. In fact, I seemed to head in the opposite direction, the East. During that time I felt as if any words or thoughts that I might write down were simply the result of an ego trying to gain further control over me. I intended to somehow obliterate my ego, in order that I might live more fully in the Present, which is all we've got. It wasn't until I read Morton's last letter a few times that I realized that my trip East was simply 'heady,' concerned only with ideas, no experience. From the neck down, I was dying. In fleeing from my Ego, I wound up getting even more entangled in its net of abstractions.

"Now, my 'head' is full and satisfied. The thirst for some kind of knowledge or truth that accompanied me from as early as I can remember up to the present is quenched. I want no more 'heady ideas' and theories. I 'know' all that is necessary and anything more would simply be extraneous.

"What I do feel to be important for my development **now** is to get in touch with my feelings, my guts! More specifically I need to Love and to allow myself to be loved. Until I met Morton my own feelings and ability to love and be loved were alien to me. After sharing my paper with Mort, I entered into the 'happiest' period of my existence thus far. I cried a lot, I felt a lot, I began to think and feel that Michael was all right. Love—damn it—it's the only 'thing' that matters in this world of ours—but it's so hard to find and express.

"I told Joan over Christmas break about Love, its importance; about how I wanted Love to be my guiding light, not \$ money \$, as it is for all too many miserable souls. [Joan is an ex-'girlfriend' and has become the closest female companion that I have.] She agreed very strongly and told me of the incredible amount of it that I'm capable of giving but don't.

"Yes, that is my task, so to speak. If I don't allow Love to enter into my life, I'll end up like my uncle and all the others. And if I get to an old age and look back upon my negligence and awry priorities, I might surely put an end to it all. Pousette Dart Band . . . 'That man knows the Spirit.' [A popular song that a band member wrote about his father.]

"I hope that someday it [the Spirit] will remain with me for longer periods of time than it does now. I feel very strongly that the richness of my life thus far (both positive and negative) was not in vain and is somewhat of an indication of what's to come."

Your quote re: how I should focus on living and meaning will

come later. Discussion about having a hard time accepting that
. . . wanting to die . . . etc. . . .

"But I haven't lived yet.

"To find oneself it is necessary to lose oneself. 'Sheer pro-
fundity,' but very true. I have never 'lost myself' entirely in
anyone or anything. I've been Prufrock in his shell.

"I'm breaking out of it again and feel that by picking up
writing again it will help me to stay somewhat on course."

Re Dreams:

"Since I thought that dreams were also ego-builders [de-
ceptions of some kind] I neglected them and didn't bother to
write them down. But now, I feel them to be important and
a vehicle through which I can become more in touch with the
'inner' Michael. Perhaps the Eastern mind can neglect dreams
and their images, but I [Western bred] can't. They have
something to say, and by paying attention to them, one is
respecting a 'force' beyond [and outside of] oneself."

Therefore I'll be writing more this semester; reflections and
dreams which most likely will lead to insights with regard to
my life. I feel this to be necessary right now if I am to become
more "whole" and a more loving person. Morton, this is only
one entry but I hope it has given you some indication of where
I'm at. It's pretty accurate although I see some kinks in my
reasoning and I would have deleted or modified parts. I've written a lot in the past two weeks and have had some extraordinary
dreaming activity. I'll be keeping it up.

One big difference in me from the last time I wrote is that I
have rekindled a sense of Hope for myself and my life.

I'll write you in a couple of weeks to fill you in on my plans
(options) for next year. Right now it looks like it's between a
year of volunteer service (maybe Jesuit Volunteer Corps) or
working as a counselor in N.Y. State Department of Services.
I'll be more specific next time I pick up the pen. For now, I've
got to hit the sack.

Love,
Michael

Another most important kind of conscious reflecting time is the time to find the priorities in one's life. The life which is not consciously directed often flows with little meaning and ends in a swamp. The planning which does not take into account the depth of one's unconscious and dream life sometimes leads to a desert and sterility. How seldom we actually stop and see how we spend our time, how we might like to spend our time, how the deepest part of us would have us spend our time!

I have discussed the matter of priorities and time in a chapter entitled "Time" in *The Other Side of Silence*. When I stop time and sit down in silence I sometimes find it helpful to see exactly how I spend my time. First of all I list the ways in which I occupy my time. Recently I made the following list:

My work, a job
My wife and family
My writing
My lecturing and teaching
My religious practice, prayer and meditation, journal writing, and time in sacramental life
My time with students and counselees, in person and on the phone
My recreation, time to rest and to play, to enjoy life, to exercise
My reading time for filling the gaps in my knowledge
My friends, keeping in touch with them by phone or in person
My sleep
My wasted time

The next step in looking at my priorities is to write down the time which I actually spend in each of these activities. I am usually shocked at the amount of time that I spend on nonessentials. In my case I find that often I have neglected time for recreation and time with my family. My actual expenditure of time is often far different from what I think it should be.

The next step is to sit down with this list in quietness, looking at my values and trying to determine how I should spend my time. Which activities deserve the most of my time? How would I ideally allocate my time?

The last stage in pulling my life together and getting it back in focus is to make plans to change my life and to spend my time as I truly want to, according to my highest values. If I do not take some positive steps in this direction I am living unconsciously, letting unseen motives determine my pattern of living rather than consciously shaping the course of my being.

At least every three months or so I need to review this list and ascertain whether my actual use of time is nearer to the ideal than it was. Another reason for this constant review is that my life changes. When children are small one's top priority should be spending time with them. Such time can never be recaptured at a later date. Often it would be wise to put off some of the time we use in personal development until we have more time later in life. If I had one thing to do over again, I would spend more time with my children and family when the children were young and needing my love and attention. Truly creative living involves such planning, in which conscious and unconscious are brought together and integrated.

In this time of conscious reflection there are hundreds of things that can be done. I can look at the people in my life and examine my reactions to them. Why am I drawn to this person or that? Why do certain people make me angry just by the way they walk across the room toward me? Why does some insignificant event cause such a violent response?

This is also a time for listing all the alternatives for college or for one's profession before making a choice. This is the time to take a look at one's job to see if it really matches one's interests and meets one's needs. Before every major decision a journal is a good friend. A plus and minus chart can be helpful, whether I am deciding on getting married, changing jobs, retiring, going on a trip, buckling down to write a book or building a house. In this chart one divides the pages of one's journal into two parts:

pluses   *minuses*
(+)   (−)

Then one writes down all the positive aspects of the prospects about which one is deciding on one side of the page and all the negative ones in the other column. Give yourself a whole hour; let the matter play around in your head and then come back and write any other negatives or positives. When you are finished you will be in a better position to make an intelligent and conscious decision. If you still feel drawn to the decision with the greater number of negatives, it probably means that you are not facing some aspect of the choice ahead.

It is very helpful to listen to dreams and to work with the depth of one's self in imaginative writing, but *it is really quite silly to do so until one has first examined the situation* consciously and carefully. Running one's life by dreams and intuitions, without using one's conscious and rational capabilities, is as foolish as trying to force one's entire life into a purely conscious and rational pattern.

Autobiographical reflections

It is nearly impossible to see the way ahead unless one has stopped and reflected on the way one has come. Many professional schools require applicants to write a short autobiography as part of their entrance requirements. They want to see the desire for professional training in the context of the whole of a person's life. It is strange how seldom we stop and look over the general pattern of our journey. Like so many aspects of our depths, the more time we spend reflecting on our past days and hours the more we are likely to remember. One's picture of the past is never completed until one dies (and perhaps not even then), for new experiences and new insights open up the locked doors of memory and give new understandings of the thread of meaning in one's life. One's autobiography is never completed. Only God knows the full meaning of my life, and only as I bring my life before the divine lover and listen will I find its ultimate significance.

There are many ways to begin an autobiography. I can simply set aside some time and try to write four to ten pages about my life and its meaning. Or I can start on one aspect of my life, my religious experience, my professional life, my hobbies, my family life, my relation to my body and sports, my sexuality. . . . The list is endless. In his book *At a Journal Workshop* Ira Progoff suggests starting with the *now*. One takes a look at the period (or general situation) in which one finds oneself. How do I feel about my life and work, about my achievements, my hopes? What are my fears and ambitions, my joys and satisfactions? The best beginning for an autobiography is knowing where I am and what I am looking for. I have found that one of the best ways to get people to start in the now is to ask them to take an hour and write the ten deepest hungers of their hearts, and then to write the ten most disturbing doubts about their faith and meaning. This opens many people to greater inner searching.

Progoff also outlines a method of looking back through life by listing the stepping-stones in one's life, the truly significant and memorable events which stand out when one stops to reflect on the past. These can be either pleasant or unpleasant. He also suggests that we limit ourselves to eight or ten and never more than twelve entries. If one does not have a limit, the list can easily become endless. After one has consciously reflected on what entries to include, one becomes very still (following the suggestions which we have given earlier). Often in this half-conscious, half-fantasy state events, pictures, voices begin to bubble up which give an additional content to our conscious reflections. Progoff calls this stepping into quietness and allowing images to appear the use of "twilight imagery." It is very important to open up the depths of ourselves by imagination and fantasy, but I believe this practice is more helpful when it is added to conscious reflection rather than when it is used alone.

After reading Progoff's suggestions I used his method of listing stepping-stones. I became quiet and listened, and the following twelve entries emerged (I saw the value of limiting the entries as I did it):

birth and childhood sickness
the sense of rejection, weakness, and sickness as an older child
the discovery of my body and sexuality
the awareness of having a good mind which could be used to gain approval in high school and college

the sickness and death of my mother and the emotional struggle of living in an alien world

the beginnings of success, in graduate school, in physical discipline, in my first parish work

marriage, relationships, and children

coming to a dead-end street, anxiety, analysis, and struggle

the discovery of the spiritual world, the significance of my
Christian faith

a period of blending spirit, mind, and body

doors opening, possibilities unfolding

These stepping-stones give structure to my life and history. I can then go back and work with any one of these
areas which needs attention. I have found that I need to go
back and work with the inner child and adolescent who are
still with me and still have an influence on me, even if I am
not aware of them. We shall give more details about how
to do this work later.

I have also found it helpful to take a look at my spiritual
experiences as Progoff suggests. Even though I had kept a
journal for many years, I had never stopped to list all those
times when it seemed that God had broken through and
touched my life. I did not write these in order, but rather
as they came to me. Here is the list which came to me in
that period of several hours of reflection:

1. praying for my mother and having her be healed at that
   time
2. Fear of the attic as a child, realization of spiritual reality
   or another dimension of reality
3. hearing of my mother's experience of being visited in a
   dream by a young man who committed suicide
4. my mother's ESP capacity of knowing if I was sick across
   the country
5. a woman being healed of inoperable cancer while I was in
   high school

   6. Max Zeller's story of escape from the Nazis

   7. delivered out of darkness, depression, and despair again and again by meditation through the risen Christ.

   8. the experience of having two analysts in Zürich give the same interpretation to my dreams

   9. finding direction out of a dead-end street through understanding of my dreams

  10. the overwhelming experience of love

  11. reading Jung's *Memories, Dreams, Reflections* alone at Newport Beach

  12. ESP experiences of someone close to me

  13. my friend Andy finding the same deliverance from darkness as I by using meditation

  14. confirmation of the same by Gloria

  15. my nightly dialog with the divine lover and the insights and wisdom which have come from these

  16. leading a group of ministers in Schenectady in meditation and having many of them experience another dimension for the first time

  17. numinous dream experiences, ESP experiences in dreams

  18. the wise direction and depth of insight of Hilde and James Kirsch

  19. reading Plato again and seeing how his thinking related to the church fathers and to shamanism

  20. reading Helen Luke's *Dark Wood to White Rose* and then reading Dante's *Divine Comedy*

  21. my children's testing me and showing me the quality of love necessary to be a follower of Christ

  22. my wife's loving care through thick and thin

  23. having the New Testament open up like a tightly closed bud as these other experiences opened my eyes to it

It would be difficult to convey how much this experience of listing these events deepened the reality of God's providence for me and how much more solid my inner life and faith were when I finished.

We can list the significant events in any aspect of our

lives. On one occasion we can look back at the development of our intellectual insight. At another time we can look back over the sexual aspect of our lives. This process can actually solve problems. A student came to me in a state of suicidal depression. He had great sexual fear. He wrote out 30 pages of his past sexual experiences and feelings and was delivered from the depression. At another time we can look back over our relationship with our bodies. We can look back over our friendships and see which have been the most meaningful and have contributed most to our growth and development. The different aspects of our lives are endless. As we pick one thread and then another we form a tapestry picture woven in the fabric of our total existence.

Recently a man in his early thirties came to talk with me. He knew that he was not living up to his creative potential. I asked him to write an account of how he had come to this situation. He wrote the following perceptive autobiographical analysis. I doubt that he would have come to these understandings without this journal writing.

My Spiritual Life:

In living with Alice during these past 6+ months, I've come to realize how much of the spiritual has been lying dormant in my life for so long a time.

I feel that the reason for this dormancy has in great part been because I've feared opening up and dealing with my inner-self; my feelings, emotions, and my spiritual nature/side.

As a young boy and into my early twenties, I was very "yielded" to the Lord and sincerely wanted to have a deeper spiritual life—but as we have discussed before, I lacked discernment. I've always had an inner spiritual awareness and in a sense, a discernment as to the depth of spiritual development potential for my life; but somehow I had been unable to activate it, unable to direct it.

I've always been hungry for more of God—I was very sincere in my search/seeking—but so often I felt I was not making headway—I'd pray, read scripture and trust God—but somehow I never seemed to break through.

Because of this (my sincerely opening myself up to God without seeming effect), this left me both disillusioned and angry. Rebellion was the result. I felt I had somehow lost my own power.

In my fundamental religious training it was customary for young people to "place all on the altar of God"—I felt I did this —perhaps to extreme; leaving me with a powerless feeling— trusting God for everything—left me powerless to possess my own will/powerless to seek what "I wanted." It's taken me a long time to see this.

In subjecting my will to God's will, I tended to lose sight of the fact that I did have a will that God respected; a will that he allowed me to have—which still could be in conformity with his overall will for my life.

My rebellion from God was both good and bad—deep down I'd say much more good because it's allowed me to feel my own inner strength and will. I was not just a puppet of God as so often I felt. I was able to face my anger at God.

God's having seemingly not directed me the way I thought he should—God's having not honored my sincere, yielded heart's life was a blessing in disguise.

I was very sensitive as a child and I still am deep down. But I've also learned not to just throw my emotions/sincerity out there in a vulnerable way. I've done this by recognizing that what I believe is the right way in which God or others are to react to me/my emotions is not necessarily in fact the proper response.

God's not having taken full control of my life is in retrospect the best thing that could have happened because it taught me that I had to act—I had to give input into my life. I could not simply let God run everything as so often is seemingly taught by fundamentalists. I had to take responsibility.

I've learned that I have to continue to seek and develop my

life—especially my inner spiritual life. This has been especially noticeable to me since I've known Alice—especially since marriage. I've seen through her the need to work on myself much more via scripture study, dreams, psychological study, prayer, etc., integrating all of these areas. I've seen Alice do this—and yes, although I've seen her weaknesses, I've also seen the inner strength she derives from it.

Yet seeing all this, I've still had difficulty applying these to my own life.

In a great part I believe this is due to recognizing Alice as being so far along in these areas in comparison to myself—in a sense she has become the authority figure and because of this, when I disagree or question her in some of these areas on occasion, a friction exists. It's sometimes caused me to have an aversion to talking to her about these areas. Yet in another sense, I feel I've also developed in some of the same areas and have some of the same spiritual and psychological viewpoints as she.

I feel that sometimes Alice does not allow me to express my own views—that if I disagree with her on certain things, her "spiritual stature" overrules my views. Because of this, I've been resistant to keeping a daily journal, praying and reading scripture together, working on my dreams, etc.

Deep down this is a silly position for me to take because I also recognize the depth of my own spiritual and psychic development. More often than not, we both hold the very same views; and our sharing and growing together can only benefit each of us.

I'm working through this and hopefully with help I'll be able to develop myself more.

I do sense my own inner depth and spiritualness, but I need to sharpen and direct it.

To summarize my near-term spiritual development—I will be trying to:

1. Actively read scripture.
2. Develop my prayer and meditative life more.
3. Keep a journal.
4. Record and study my dreams.

5. Study more of Jungian psychology. (I've come to realize that Jung's ideas are so very close to my own feelings about our existence/life journey—His theories are sensing, not sterile as so much of psychology is.)

Career:

My future career choice has been intertwined with my spiritual seeking. I've wanted so much to find a deep spiritual life and often I've felt my career should be oriented in the spiritual-theological or counseling area—in helping others—

Yet there has also been a pull toward the material—not so much in the sense of acquiring wealth, but in the sense of being in the secular life, functioning effectively in that realm—yet being deeply spiritual at the same time and continuing to grow in the spiritual area while living in the secular.

In a sense it is a test for me to successfully pass my qualifying exam—and I'm feeling more and more strongly about this.

I think that in great part, my difficulty in firmly deciding and succeeding in a secular career stems from my inner spiritual needs—the lack of a totally settled inner life.

I believe that once this is consistently accomplished, I'll feel much better, much more comfortable in my career.

I've completed one year of law school and at this time I feel that I should continue with law. I'd like to obtain my law degree, pass the bar exam, and then most likely combine a law and counseling practice with Alice.

In obtaining a law degree, I'd receive a J.D. law/doctorate which would allow me to study at a Jungian institute in the future if I so choose. I also have the M.A. in counseling background to draw upon as need be.

I guess I can't really separate the inner spiritual from the secular in my life. There are those two sides of interest within me, and I've felt pulling from both.

Sometimes the law environment is unsettling since it often lacks the human sensitivity. It only looks at the surface issues—it fails to truly probe the most important inner issues of man—the issues of the heart and soul. The study is quite interesting but it lacks something quite often.

Yet I can also see where living life only in the psychology field can also have its drawbacks—often people in the field fail to responsibly face important issues involving our world. They are into such a deep inner journey that virtually everything else passes them by, and they often become incapable of functioning effectively in the real world (whatever that may be).

I'd like to strike a happy medium for myself—by doing so, I feel that I can be more effective for myself and others than simply choosing one or the other areas exclusively.

(Yet there is the pull toward one or the other area periodically, and I think this will occasionally occur throughout life.)

But I believe that if I can develop my inner spiritual life journey to a greater degree, then I can function effectively in both, and I'll satisfy both of these areas within me. I need help in assisting me with maintaining this balance.

Social:

I believe that the social areas in our relationship are slowly coming together. We are beginning to feel comfortable with entertaining and being entertained by other couples/friends.

We are getting out to see movies, dine out, ski (3 or 4 times so far this season), etc.

Alice has developed a liking for golf and she indicated she'd like to take some lessons (Golf is very contemplative and I think we both enjoy this aspect.).

I feel that for a while the adjustment to married life was sometimes a little difficult for each of us. We had to be consistently considerate of another person over a 24-hour period, 7 days a week.

For myself, I'm beginning to experience a deepening love for Alice, a sober recognition that each of us has chosen one another as a lifetime partner. I'm sensing her love for me very much.

I'm also coming to realize how much I've needed a deeply committed person loving me. I feel this from Alice.

This deepening feeling, the reality of seeing our married life unfolding before us, is frankly quite exciting. Decorating and landscaping our home, planning for a child, etc., all bring about very positive feelings within me—We are one.

There have been times when I haven't felt close sexually with
Alice. I'm coming to realize that it has stemmed from some of
the frictions that occur between two people trying to adjust to
one another. I've sometimes gone to bed with things bothering
me and it has affected my sexuality. But I think this area is being
resolved because of the deepening love feelings I'm experiencing.
The goodness of our relationship is drawing me into a closer
emotional and physical relationship with Alice.

I've come to realize that you love someone on one level when
you first marry; but as you really get to know them in marriage
and see their strengths and weaknesses, you love them even
more deeply. Not for their strengths or weaknesses, but for who
they are as a person. I'm feeling this way about Alice.

I think it takes some time to establish your identity as a couple; and as we are beginning to do this, we are beginning to
interact with others socially as well.

In essence, I believe that our social life together and our relationship with each other is improving and is moving in the
right directions. We are not without problems, but neither do I
see any real obstacles to overcome.

9

The Power of
the Imagination

IMAGINATION REVEALS and changes both the physical and spiritual worlds. One of the greatest modern philosophers of science, Paul Feyerabend, emphasizes the value of imagination in science. He states that scientific creativity and inventiveness depend more on a developed imagination than on logic and reason. He believes scientists must be trained to use their imagination if they are to come to significant scientific discovery.

What is true of the physical, material world is even more true as one begins to deal with the spiritual world. Spiritual discovery, making a direct and creative encounter with spiritual reality, may well depend on developing one's imaginative capacities. We have two hemispheres of the brain, one dealing with logic and language and the other with images, shapes, art, and story. If we are to be whole people we need to learn to use both sides of the brain and deal with our imaginative capacities. The images arising from the depths of us in dreams or fantasies or intuitions are one way by which we are brought into contact with the spiritual world. Without the use of images and imagination it is nearly impossible to obtain knowledge of the depth of ourselves or of the spiritual reality beyond us. Without imagination it is also difficult to change the direction of that inner world if we find that danger lies ahead.

I have written *The Other Side of Silence* on the use of imagination in praying and meditating. Those who would study the subject in depth are referred to Chapters 12, 13, 14, and 16 of that book. I offer the following suggestions to those who wish to develop the imagination so that it can be used creatively in journaling. These suggestions may help them deal with spiritual reality to begin to bring the depths of themselves to God for transformation.

1. It is necessary at least to entertain the possibility that in dealing with the imagination we are dealing with a reality as powerful and important as that revealed in the outer world by the five senses.

2. We must have a time and place where we will not be interrupted. Once the flow of imagination is broken by outer interference it is difficult to set it free again.

3. We need to be quiet and practice what is necessary to bring detachment from the other concerns of our lives. We will want to use the suggestions for getting quiet outlined in Chapter 3 again and again. Creative use of images and imagination seldom occurs except when we have first become still and detached.

4. Once we are quiet we can either watch the images which bubble up before us or place an image on the stage of our inner being. Once these images have the center of the stage they usually begin to have a life of their own.

5. Now we can watch these inner figures. We can observe how they move and act. We can enter the picture

and talk with them or gently lead them in the direction which seems creative and fulfilling.

6. When the situation presents more than we know how to cope with, we can introduce the Christ figure to give advice or take charge of this situation. He may show us how we can turn it around, and then we can guide our inner story in that new direction.

7. We can record this experience as it is happening or we can take time after the experience is over to set down what we have seen and done. Here we need to follow what method is best for us. I find that writing or typing helps the images flow, but some find that everything stops if they try to write and imagine at the same time.

Jung tells the story of an artist who had great difficulty in learning to use his imagination. He tried all sorts of things, and then one day while waiting for the train in the station in Zürich he noticed a colorful poster on the wall. It pictured a scene in the Alps with snowcapped mountains in the distance, a waterfall at one side, and a green hill in the foreground with cows grazing on it. He imagined that he was in the picture. He walked up among the cows to the top of the hill. The moment that he went over the brow of the hill he was stepping into another dimension of reality by using his imagination. He discovered that the same series of images came to him each time he imaginatively went over the edge of the hill. The moment he doubted the value of what he was doing, the images disappeared.

I have used this story with groups to enable them to explore their imaginative powers. Different people see very different things as they step over the edge of their inner hill. Some find a cliff and abyss, others a river or a city below, and still others walk down the other side of the hill and find a path which leads them on to all sorts of adventures. What we find tells us a great deal about who and where we are at the moment. What we do with what we find can shape our lives toward creativity, stability, or difficulty.

We change this inner world of ours whenever we consciously enter it. If we think this is peculiar, it is helpful to remember that we change the paths of electrons by observing them. One can change that world as surely as building or excavating or blasting can change the outer world. We can change both worlds for good or ill. It is important to know the center and core of meaning of that inner world so that we can work with it and not against it.

We discover a significant truth at this point. As we bring the creative power of a divine lover to bear on the events and figures of the inner world, changes often begin to take place in the inner world, in our attitudes and moods, and at the same time in the outer world. Sometimes our imagination will direct us to make changes in the outer world, and changes in the inner world do not take place until the outer changes are made. It appears, indeed, that any final change in the outer world will be preceded by a change in the world of spiritual reality, of inner images and symbols. There is power and mystery in imagination which is beyond our comprehension. We also have more power over our destinies than we sometimes think.

Dialoging with inner figures

We human beings are far more complex than we ordinarily believe. Our inner self is more like a committee than a single, simple individual. Plato wrote about the charioteer and the black and white horses of the soul. Jung has described the truth that each man has a feminine side and each woman a masculine side. He has described many other figures which he calls *archetypes*.

In one period of inward turning in my journal I imagined that I was alone in a mountain cabin. It was "a dark and stormy night" and I heard a knock on my door. I opened it to find a handsome youth drenched to the skin. After he had changed his clothes and warmed himself there was another knock, and then another. Within an hour I found nine people inside my cabin. They were inner figures I knew from my dreams and inner reflections. In addition to the youth there was a matronly woman and her crying child, a beautiful and seductive maiden, a warrior, a court jester, a scholar, a kingly figure, and a blacksmith (see Chapter V of my book, *Discernment, A Study in Ecstasy and Evil*).

These nine figures represent parts of me, aspects of my inner being. All of us have similar inner figures which represent our sexuality, our power drive, our inner hurt child, our anger and aggressiveness. And then we have some special aspects which are unique to each of us. In my case there is the scholar and the poetic youth. In my fantasy I found that I could not control these figures by myself. They were stronger than I. I needed help and so I called on Christ to come to help me. He came and brought order to my inner chaos. I have found that only he is able to coach these inner actors so that they can present a meaningful drama. Only then can my life have a consistent meaning and show the love and creativity which I would have it show.

I find that I get into trouble when one of these inner figures tries to take over the role of director and lord it over the others. Then my life is chaotic, becomes unconscious, and falls into patterns which are evil. Evil can well be described as any secondary good trying to take the place of the ultimate good. When I do not deal with my inner figures and try to bring them to Christ for direction and guidance I usually do the things that I wish I would not do and leave undone the things that I ought to do.

At conferences I find that most people can become quiet and get in touch with several important inner figures. If you have never tried it, take some time, become quiet, and see who these inner figures might be in you. You do not have to have nine. You may find five or seven. It is good to keep a limit of ten or twelve at the most.

If I am going to keep these inner parts of myself from taking over my life, I must know them and recognize the signs of their presence. When I am not myself, usually one of these inner characters has taken over the show. There are times when I am angry and destructive and there is no outer reason to be that way. The inner warrior has taken over. I may be moody, silent, or irritable; the inner maiden has taken over. I can be frightened and childish, and then the child has taken over. When I get hopelessly rational, cold and distant, the scholar has taken over as in C. S. Lewis' novel, *That Hideous Strength* (Macmillan, 1965). My blacksmith can make instruments of destruction. When I take nothing seriously, the jester is in control. When I am irresponsible and not working for my goals, the inner youth is running the show.

Each of these characters can also contribute much to me, when he or she does not try to run my life. The child can contribute wonder and new life; the youth, enthusiasm;

the warrior can protect me and my values; the matron can bring warmth and concern; the maiden can be like Dante's Beatrice, leading me to the very gates of heaven with devotion and love; the scholar can give reason and substance to my life; the court jester can contribute humor; the smith can make plowshares and pruning hooks. Only as these inner actors play their proper role in the drama of my life can they be creative. Otherwise they are likely to run off with the show and bring tragedy.

It is very important that we know ourselves. Once we have found out who some of our inner figures are, we can talk with them. Only as we get to know them can we keep them playing their proper roles. One of the most important characters for us to know is our inner child. Few of us have had truly happy, satisfactory experiences of childhood. If we do not deal with this inner hurt child, he or she (as the case may be) may keep us from any adult relationship by demanding that he or she be cared for. Or this inner child may fill us with fear of the outside adult world. One of the finest descriptions of dealing with the inner child is found in Christina Baldwin's book, *One to One: Self-Understanding Through Journal Writing* (M. Evans, 1977). In it she shares her own struggle with her inner child.

How do we go about talking with our inner child? Again we must be reminded of the need to set aside time, to become quiet, and to imagine the inner child within us as being before us. I had thought about my inner child, but had never spoken directly to that child. Last summer I did. In my prayer time the inner voice suggested I talk to the inner child. I called to mind a picture of me as a child, of a nine or ten-year-old sitting forlornly at the edge of a fountain. I spoke to that child:

ME: You sit there so forlornly at the fountain's edge. Why are you so sad?

CHILD: I will talk with anyone who will talk with me, but no one seems to want to talk with me or spend time with me, not even you. Isn't that a good reason to be sad? After all these years you look at me.

ME: How old are you?

CHILD: I'm eight or nine or ten or eleven. It makes no difference. I am the same hurting child.

ME: Why do you hurt so much?

CHILD: Because no one loves me. I'm a nuisance to everyone and even to you. You see me projected out in others and take care of them, but you do not see me or deal with me or treat my hurt. Some of your friends see me and are kind to me, but Mother and Father are too busy. They do not think I have any potential. I don't fit into the mold. They fear that I will never amount to anything. Sometimes I think that Father loves me, but he is afraid. Are you afraid of me, too? Are you going to reject me, too?

ME *(turning to the inner voice)*: Lord, how do I let him know that I love him?

INNER VOICE: First you need to recognize that he is there and then you can spend time with him. Reach out to him, take him in your arms, and then bring him to me.

(I reach out a hand. The child puts his hand in mine. His face brightens.)

CHILD: Let's walk and talk. Do you really love me? Do you really want me to be with you? I'm afraid you'll take me up and then drop me. That would be worse than no friendship at all.

ME: I'll try to be faithful to you as I have been to some of my friends. I'm afraid that you really don't want me either and that you will drop me. You look so pure and I'm soiled by the world. I'm also fearful that you will cling to me and control my life and take away my freedom.

CHILD: So, you too are afraid.

ME: Yes, I am afraid. Without Christ I could not manage my
life at all. Do you see him standing there behind the
wall? He would take your other hand. He has taught
me what love is.

*(I point to Christ, who stands there. The child nods that he
would like to go, and we move over toward him. The child
reaches out a hand. Christ picks him up and embraces him. He
suggests that we go to a beautiful swimming hole up on Wild
Creek. It is a beautiful summer day, and we are suddenly there
and swim in the cool water and dry ourselves in the sun on the
rocks. Then Christ tells me not to be afraid to let him into my
heart, and he disappears. The child comes over and lies down
beside me with his head on my chest. I speak to him. . . .)*

ME: How beautiful you are, my lad, how beautiful and loving
and seeking love. You would love me, who have wanted
love.

CHILD: I love you just as you are, all of you. I trust you. Never
fear my ceasing to love. I have looked for ages for this
very moment. I could not reject you. Just do not leave me.

ME: I'll be as faithful as I can be.

CHILD: I feel new hope. I dare look into myself. I feel strange
stirrings in me that I fear no one can understand.

ME: I understand. I know you well and love you. . . .

*(Then we fall silent. The sun begins to set and the sky is a riot
of color. I feel warm, alive, and glad.)*

Some time later I realized that there was an inner adolescent who needed my concern. I knew when I concluded
the dialog with the child that there was another I needed to
talk with—the inner youth, the adolescent. Getting ready to
write and writing had taken the better part of two hours,
and so the next day I set aside some more time and I returned. I pictured in my mind the teenager coming home
after school, sitting alone on the front porch, wondering
about sexuality and friendship, about school and the life
ahead, feeling as though no one would listen to his confu-

sion and turmoil. I watched him for a while from behind the shrubs at the corner of the house, and then I stepped out and spoke to him.

ME: Hi, you look as though you would like to talk, and so I thought I would step up and pass the time of day. I hope I'm not intruding.

YOUTH: Heavens, no, I'm so glad you stopped. I've longed for it and you have ignored me. But how do I know you won't make fun of me or be ashamed of me? I'm so alone. I have no one I can talk with. I have only known rejection, separation, and the confusion of a growing life. I live in a house where sexuality is considered evil and I feel it bursting through my being. I don't know which way to go or how to show hostility. They tell me that I'm bright, and what good does that do when there is so little satisfaction, so much aloneness.

ME: I have listened to many youths, and many of them tell the same story. Adults so seldom understand their inner warfare. Even though I have not talked with you, I knew that you were there and I have tried to give understanding to the other youths who needed it. I guess I was afraid to deal with you. I loved you so much I was afraid.

YOUTH: That is hard to believe. I feel so alone.

ME: You need to be alone no longer. I acknowledge you as my own and I want you to know how much I love you.

YOUTH: Come to my room where we can have some privacy. I want to show you something and talk where no other can hear.

(We go to his room. He begins to pour out his pain and hurt, his sexual experimentation. He shows me books on sex, some he is ashamed of and others not as much. He pours out his story of fear and separation. It goes on and on. We are sitting on a couch together and I put my arms around him and he continues on. Then he weeps. I hardly know what to do, and I call Christ to come and help me deal with the youth.)

ME: What can I do, Lord? How can I heal him?

CHRIST: Give him love. Reassure him. There is nothing wrong with him. He has been damaged by a puritanical society and given no encouragement or love or understanding, only criticism and rejection. Stay with him, listen to him. He has great gifts. The hurt he has experienced has enabled you to listen to others like him. It is he who led you to me.

(For a long time I simply hold the youth. He has needed affection so much. We talk on long into the night, or rather I listen long into the night and then we go for a walk in the moonlit, clear summer night. Having expressed all his fear and shame and confusion, we turn to other things. He tells me of poems he has written, of ideas which are bubbling through his head, of hopes for the future. He tells me that he would like to write. We finally return to his room. His gloom has lifted. He banters with jokes and tells me funny things he has done. And then quite happily he goes to bed. I embrace him and go my way. In conclusion he says:)

YOUTH: Thank you so much for coming. I have needed you for so long. Please come again and talk longer. Don't forget me. I need you.

ME: My friend, thank you for sharing so much of yourself with me. You have trusted me and have made me a better person. We shall meet again and I will not forget you.

These are two conversations which have been very meaningful. These conversations need to be repeated again and again if I am to bring more healing to these inner parts of me. One can talk with any of one's inner figures. I have often talked with the various aspects of my inner femininity (the "anima," as Jung called it). Jung used to say that he would have long conversations with "Miss Jung," and this kept him conscious of who and what he was. At different times one can discuss different things with these inner parts of one's self and one can always learn something new, be given new insights, and come to new integration.

It is so much easier to talk to inner figures than abstractions like sexuality or anger or intelligence. These inner figures are real, and as we get to know them and work with them in the presence of Christ he gradually helps us become what we are capable of becoming. We are made into the image of the likeness of Christ. God cannot do much with us when we present him false faces, but only when we bring all of us, all parts of us, as best we can. Then we begin the process of transformation which has no end.

Many people have found a journal to be a way of discovering and dealing with themselves. Sometimes the inner figures appear as animals or insects rather than people. A very capable woman in her early fifties wrote the following description of how she got into journal keeping and then into conversation with her inner figures and her guide, Christ.

My spiritual advisor led me into journal writing as a means of getting in touch with unfamiliar parts of myself, as well as with God. Over and over for a year or more, he suggested that I keep a journal in which I would write down thoughts, feelings, and dreams. I resisted for a long time, but finally I began. For a year I made sporadic efforts at putting down some of my feelings. When I reread these pages I realize what a huge burden of anger I was hauling around with me.

Then I recorded a dream in which a stranger came up my driveway to the back door of my house. He wanted to talk to me, but I wouldn't let him in; I didn't quite trust him. Although I didn't want to run away from him as I had in previous dreams, I would only talk to him through the screen door. I told my advisor about the dream, and he said, "Talk to the stranger. He is not only part of you, he may also be a Christ figure." That seemed a bit farfetched, but at the same time I had a feeling he was right; so I tried it.

I held an imaginary conversation with that stranger; on paper I wrote it all down, what I said to him and what he said to me.

And my advisor was right. The inner stranger was and is a pathway to Christ for me, and we have been carrying on conversations—usually one-sided ones because I keep forgetting to listen—ever since.

My journal is my self-portrait. It is the means of grace by which Christ has enabled me to come into his presence to confront myself and to learn to know him.

August 20

GINNY: . . . I'm not repentant, I'm just having a good time being remorseful. I'm telling myself how wonderful I am in being so honest with myself and confessing all this to you. But I'm enjoying it . . . (as I enjoy other people's suffering)—I feed on other people's sufferings. . . . It all nourishes some dark loathsome part of me.

CHRIST: Beloved, that's enough. There's no darkness that I cannot lighten. I know your darkness, better than you do.

GINNY: Then why do you stay? Why do you tell me you love me when you couldn't love me? No one can love anything so dark and stinking.

CHRIST: I loved Lazarus when he was dead and stinking. I called him forth from corruption to life. As I call you forth from corruption to life.

GINNY: My insides are slimy white grubs—maggots.

CHRIST: Give me one of them. There. See it walk across my hand.

GINNY: It's changing color, Lord, it's not white and dead anymore. It's not slimy, either. It's fuzzy; it's spinning its slime into thread. It's making a cocoon. It wasn't a maggot—it was a caterpillar.

CHRIST: Yes, love. The maggots that eat you in the darkness can become caterpillars in my light.

GINNY: And then butterflies?

CHRIST: Eventually, after they have slept in their cocoons. They need time in their cocoons to sleep and grow.

GINNY: Thank you, Christ. I'll try. I'll keep holding the maggots to your light.

Dialoging with outer figures and situations

Just as one can talk with parts of one's self, one can also talk with actual outer figures, both living and dead. Most of us have used the practice of writing letters to people who offend us, who made us angry, or to people to whom we would express love. We never intended to send these letters. One can then write back the letter which one would imagine that the other would return in response. In this way one can often see what one feels and thinks, and often much is expressed in the letters from the other which we had never thought of before. This kind of writing gives clarity, objectivity, and distance. One can get much the same effect by imagining that one is talking to the other person and recording what is said by both. It is an inner dialog or drama.

And who are the ones with whom I might dialog? Of course the first group of people who come to mind are those within one's family—mother, father, brothers and sisters, spouse, children, and relatives. We can learn much about ourselves and our relationships in these dialogs. One can also dialog with friends and enemies, employers and employees, or any important other. *So often we do not really know what we feel until we have written something of this sort.* We simply do not know all that is within us until we stop and look. Seldom do we know what we are until we disclose ourselves to another. A journal provides this kind of self-disclosure.

Recently I have gone through the difficult experience of having to break up the family home. Some years after my father died, my stepmother died. I cannot express how helpful it was to have conversations with my stepmother and my father. These are very personal and not the kind of thing which can or should be shared, but they brought me to a new perspective, helped me appreciate the good things which these people had done and forgive their faults, and so untie myself from them and let them go. Our hatred often ties us to people more than our love, and how silly it is to be tied to those whom we dislike! This kind of writing can help us to look at others in the light of Christ.

My mother died when I was 21. She was the daughter of a Presbyterian minister and the granddaughter of one. She was deeply stamped with the Puritanism and Victorianism of the late 19th century. She was very loving and kind and had a tremendous influence on my life. Some time ago I realized that I needed to talk with her. I imagined her in her prime. We were both adults and were walking along the brook which led past the church in the town we lived in when I was a child. I spoke to her.

ME: Mother, I know you mean well, but you have certainly burdened me with rejection, dependence, devaluation of the body and sexuality, and given me a horrible sense of sin. I love you nonetheless, even though at times I am very angry at you and the evil which used you. But you also gave me the only love I had in childhood.

MOTHER: As I told you not long before I died, it would have served me right if you had totally rejected me and ignored me.

ME: That I could never do. I am not in any position to reject anyone. First you rejected me and turned me over to the maids; and then when you were alone with no one else caring for you, you overloved me, adding one sin to another. But there seems to be no way to raise children properly. . . . I have lived out much of your repressed life. Can I be freed from it?

MOTHER: There is more to our relationship than you say in your anger, but be as angry as you wish. You will not make me sick or upset me now. It is good for both of us to be honest. This will help to free both of us.

ME: Why haven't I done this before?

MOTHER: Even without coming to this direct confrontation you have come to understand the real situation and you have come to real creativity. This meeting brings to fruition the work that you have done. It is the icing on the cake. I am proud of you. You have done well. Thank you for carrying what I put on you unconsciously and still loving me. You, too, are a loving person.

ME: You don't want me tied to you emotionally, do you?

MOTHER: It keeps me back, as well as you.

ME: How do we get disengaged?

MOTHER: By talking like this, facing the deep love and fear and anger we have for one another and loving each other for each other's growth.

ME: How much of my compulsion is identification with you?

MOTHER: It is more than this. Our relationship opened you to the archetypal world and its fascination, but your compulsions have a deeper root than personal relationship.

ME *(speaking to the Christ):* Lord, if I must bear these inner tensions I bear them as my cross. Help with the sacrifice.

CHRIST: Be careful what you sacrifice. More growth and maturity will come, but growth is difficult and sometimes painful. Keep at it. But don't let Myra, your mother, stand there alone.

ME: Mother, Myra, friend, you kept me alive, but loused up my life. I have real ambivalence toward you, real love, real anger. . . .

MOTHER: I understand. I'm sorry I was so ignorant and confused and passed it on. The evil one did a good job on me, too. I feel with you the pain you bear. I didn't face the split within me and it killed me. You have borne the pain. I am sorry for some of the inheritance I gave you, yet I love you and died for you—as did our Lord. . . .

(I open my arms to her and we embrace. I feel her love and concern and I feel mine flowing out to her.)

ME: I ask your continued help and guidance from your perspective on the other side. Help me stay close to my Lord. I know you have continued with me and given me guidance after your death.

MOTHER: I love you and I have tried to make up for the damage that I have caused, to open doors and even give inspiration from time to time.

ME: Thank you for this time together. Thank you for your love and concern. Thank you so much for those words about your rejection of me as a child before you died.

MOTHER: I love you, my son, my friend, my companion. Remember that there is a great difference between what I was, what I am now, and what your image of me was and is. Let us meet again. We are on the same path.

It would be difficult to convey the freedom and release that this conversation provided. It gave me a new perspective on my life and reconciled much of my ambivalence.

In addition to speaking to the important people in one's life, one can also speak to situations of the past. One can speak to one's marriage, one's job, one's hobby, or nearly any aspect of one's life. Progoff suggests listing the situations and events which have been most significant to you and then dialoging with them. A friend of mine spent some time with a group which was exploring journaling as a way of inner growth. He is a very successful businessman, but he had never really looked at his marriage and how he got into it. The following dialog gave him objectivity and helped him work more creatively on his marriage.

ME: Well, wedding, I'm not quite sure what it is you and I have to say to one another. You certainly were the official kicking off point for something very significant in

my life. And you have many brothers and sisters impact-
ing the lives of others.

WEDDING: Yes, that was a special day—my day! **You and**
Dorothy brought a nice crowd to *my* wedding that day.

ME: I agree, there were all our good friends and our families
and acquaintances. I'm glad you enjoyed them.

WEDDING: Date, time and place—June 29, 1962, 11:00 A.M.
Yes, you were just barely there, I recall; but your wife
really had it all planned and put together. All you had to
do was show up and look appropriately happy.

ME: I may have looked that way, but oh boy I sure didn't feel
that way. I was scared stiff and was asking myself every
step if I really wanted to be part of your big show.

WEDDING: And what did you decide?

ME: There was no choice at that time. There could be no
change!

WEDDING: If you had it to do over today, what would it be
like?

ME: Well, I'd spent a lot more time knowing myself and I'd
have a lot harder time deciding to "go ahead with it."

WEDDING: And would you still have a wedding?

ME: I doubt if I would live alone, but I might choose to have
women friends without all the entangling alliances.

WEDDING: You like that freedom and independence?

ME: Yes, I suppose I would—at least for awhile.

WEDDING: Well, that's way out of my field. My area is getting folks together, not pushing them apart. Well, so
long. . . .

ME: But I—wait, don't you offer any alternative?

WEDDING: Nope, I'm a wedding—either you have me or
you don't, so—see you around.

ME: (Sigh)—so long. I sure wish I knew if I really want you
around or not!

Turning moods into images

Emotions and moods are difficult to deal with. Often they
possess us, and when we try to deal with them they slip

through our fingers like quicksilver. The more we try to get a handle on them, the more they elude us. In addition our emotions of fear and anger, depression and self-importance often separate us from God like a wall of rock. Even our moods of joy and ecstasy, of rejoicing and insight pass and are gone if we do not record them. After they vanish we can be left in a dry place.

Is there any way that we human beings can begin to take control of these emotions? Is there any way we can keep the negative moods from drawing us into destructiveness and darkness? Is there a method by which we can give substance to our times of joy at the nearness of God?

There is a way which I learned from Dr. Jung and which I have been using for nearly 30 years. Dr. Jung's autobiography describes how he dealt with the great waves of emotion which washed over him as he confronted the unconscious after his break with Freud. First of all he used certain exercises to quiet himself. He used Yoga exercises, but instead of using them to obliterate all emotions and images, he used them only so that he could quiet himself and deal with the psychic contents and images which were sweeping over him.

Jung concluded: "To the extent that I managed to translate the emotions into images—that is to say, to find the images which were concealed in the emotions—I was inwardly calmed and reassured. Had I left those images hidden in the emotions, I might have been torn to pieces by them. There is a chance that I might have succeeded in splitting them off; but in that case I would inexorably have fallen into a neurosis and so been ultimately destroyed by them anyhow. As a result of my experiment I learned how helpful it can be, from the therapeutic point of view, to find the particular images which lie behind emotions." *

I find that in addition to turning the mood into the image, I need to lead the emotion to a positive resolution. In accomplishing this change I find the image of the risen Christ of enormous help, for here is one who has conquered death, fear, darkness, derision, meaninglessness, pain, and evil. There is nothing that I cannot bring before this one, nothing that he cannot help me with. *However, he cannot help me with what I will not face within myself.* Moods and destructive emotions are often symptoms of deep inner conflict. These must be confronted if they are to be changed. I realized this truth on a spring day as my wife and I were driving through the country around Holland, Michigan. I knew that I needed to listen to the depths and so she drove, kept still, and allowed me to deal with the inner darkness which I was experiencing.

ME: The darkness is tugging at me from the center; the lead
　　　ball is hanging from the depth of me, inner weariness,
　　　inner hopelessness.
DARK VOICE: All is hopeless, all vain. Curl up and die.
ME: You have me in your grasp again so that a large part of
　　　me would like to give up. You are very seductive. You
　　　speak within and make me think that I am speaking.
　　　The deadly poppies lure me to sleep and death. There is
　　　a murmuring within: "Go to sleep and die."
DARK VOICE: There is no meaning or value. All is lost and
　　　vain, hopeless. There is only matter, no purpose, all vain,
　　　creep into thy narrow bed, creep, let no more be said.

---

* C. G. Jung, *Memories, Dreams, Reflections* (Pantheon, 1963), p. 177. The relationship between emotions and images has been explored in depth by James Hillman in his excellent book, *Emotion* (Northwestern Univ., 1964). I have discussed the same material in Chapter 6 of my book *Can Christians Be Educated?* (Religious Education Press, 1977), "Education for Understanding Emotion and Finding Value."

. . . Strew on her roses, roses, in quiet she reposes, ah, would that you did, too. . . .

ME: The siren voice calls me. The task seems so hard, life so difficult, so futile, the darkness attractive, the endless rest is not me but the darkness being seductive, destructive and seductive, and speaking from within.

DARK VOICE: Give up and sleep, pull the plug. . . .

ME: What, Lord, do I do?

VOICE: Go with it and see where it leads you.

(I enter the silence and see and follow a beautiful buxom woman into the poppy field. She dances ahead of me, young and beautiful. As I go on I realize that the fumes of the poppies are overcoming me, but I go on and the sweet fumes overpower me and I collapse. As I fall I see a mask fall from the woman's face and I see that behind the mask is a death's head. I fall to the ground, but I do not lose consciousness. Rather my consciousness is separated from my body and I watch my body from outside. Elves emerge from a hole in the ground near my body. The deadly woman points to my body. They laugh with glee and come dancing around the body which lies there amid the poppies. They rip off my clothes and jab the body with knife-sharp sticks and pitchforks. I am separated from it, yet I must stay with it; and I can faintly feel that they are doing all this to me. They perpetrate every vileness upon this body of mine. I wonder why they want to do this. Their jabs reach to the heart of the body. Then they hack up the body into little pieces and then carry the pieces of it back into their underground place. There it will rot and they will feed it to the soil. The woman has adjusted her mask and has gone out to lure other unsuspecting travelers into the field of poppies with her plaintive song.)

ME: Lord, I have followed it through. Here I am, lost and fragmented, my spirit cut off from my rotting body. What now? How can this be redeemed? Why the pain again and again?

INNER VOICE: Your busyness has opened you to the destructive and seductive voices once again. You have tried to save the whole world and have lost yourself. In turning your mood into an image you have simply allowed yourself to realize consciously what has already happened unconsciously. This is why the inner pain and darkness must be faced through. It has already happened. The mood of darkness is the reflection of an inner event which has already taken place. The seduction took place over these last weeks when you thought that you could do more than a human being. Until you stepped into that mood and realized the reality of what had already taken place within you, I could not turn it around for you. The imagination brings you to the reality of your inner being, to what is actually there, to what has already taken place. I can only change reality when it is acknowledged.

ME: Lord, this is where I am, torn, broken, fragmented. Help! Help!

(There is a blinding light, a lightning strike, a crash of thunder. The earth hears and trembles and spits out the pieces of me, rotten, stinking, like excrement. . . .)

ME: And what can you do with these rotting fragments?

INNER VOICE: Quiet, child, I made you and I can remake you.

(He takes the pieces in his hand and it is like a million spiders weaving webs. . . . Out of the rotting fragments emerges a body, a better body than before. He calls to me. . . .)

INNER VOICE: Come, child, inhabit this body again and be whole.

(As he holds that body of mine, I return so that I can feel his loving embrace, the embrace of the creator, lover, transformer, redeemer. . . . I realize that he has carried me again to the pool which lies at the foot of the cliff from which the spring flows. The sun is sinking and I rest and sleep. He holds me close until morning when I awake and am alive again. Here is the perfectly whole one, union of opposites. We laugh and play. We come down to the sea and the white sand. Naked we play in the warm waves, and they renew me more and more. Then we walk up along the beach to the cottage which stands on the

*rock above the ocean. The sun is setting as he leads me up to it.
The cool wind comes up from the sea. He gives me a tunic of
lambskins and lights a fire on the hearth. We laugh and talk.)*

ME: Even though I am a lecherous and egocentric fool, you
still love me, Lord? I do not understand why you
continue to care and help me when I call. I am not
worthy. . . .

INNER VOICE: Child, who is to say how worthy anything is
but me? I know your condition. I loved Peter who de-
nied me and Paul who persecuted me. You are trying
and you live close to the precipice, to the abyss. You have
grown much. Keep trying. My love is forever. Rest in my
love. Speak it forth.

ME: I'll try. Please, Lord, pick me up again when I fall. Continue with me.

The secret of such writing is to be still and enter the mood
or emotion which besets one. One savors it and tries to describe what it is like, what it feels like. Sometimes one tries
for half an hour to milk the central image out of the mood.
One picture after another comes, but does not quite fit; and
then an image emerges which one knows is right. One follows the picture which unfolds. One follows the darkness
down, down to whatever destructive place one is led.

The problem with most existential writing is that the
authors leave one in the pit. Sartre glories that he leaves you
in the meaningless, absurd abyss and laughs. Camus finds
himself in the same dead-end street, but he continues seeking and finds no way out. Most modern literature (from
The Women's Room to the recent articles on depression in
Psychology Today) simply assume that there can be no
meaning, no life after death, no transformation. It is relatively easy to express depression and hopelessness. Beckett's
Waiting for Godot is such convincing meaninglessness.

Most modern human beings have forgotten that one can

go down into the pit and still pass through to the other side. The psalmists constantly talked about the pit, but even before the time of Christ, before he came and wrote hope into the fabric of history, the psalmists fought on through until they found light.

If one is to find light, victory, and meaning, then one needs to struggle on through the darkness until some light appears. *One seldom finds the light unless one has at least a hypothesis that there is some light, that victory can be found.* Very, very seldom does one find gold in a mountain range until one has enough hope to take the necessary risks involved in looking for it. I have already stated the value of the institutional church, which holds up the possibility of hope. There is practically no other agency in society which offers the hope of transcendental transformation and victory. What one does not believe is possible, one often fails to see. Bruner and Postman did an experiment with a deck of cards containing a red six of spades. People viewing the deck of cards containing this anomalous card did not see its uniqueness *because they did not expect to see it.* In our time it is as strange to believe in a divine lover standing ready to help floundering human beings as it is to expect to see a red six of spades.

If we are to turn negative emotions and moods into creative images, we need first to have the courage to face the depths of our selves and find the actual condition existing there. Even though this is painful, the truth will come out sooner or later. It is better to face our darkness when life is going along fairly well than when we are immobilized through depression or a broken leg or pneumonia. Then we need to consider the possibility that there is some way out of the chaos. And we wonder what will happen if we fail to find victory on the other side of defeat. We will certainly be no worse off than if we simply sit and stew in the blackness of the pit. And then slowly and resolutely we need to nudge our inner figures on through the darkness and toward the light. We seize on every bit of light and see where it takes us.

Fortunately or unfortunately, the Lord of light and love is very polite. He seldom comes where he is not invited. One needs to reach out again and again and call out again and again until there is some response. If one continues, a response nearly always comes.

A friend of mine was struggling through a perfectly ghastly inundation by the unconscious. He was only 21, and he had opened himself to it by the use of hallucinogenic drugs. Once one is opened in this way, it is usually impossible to close off the unconscious; then one has the monumental task of confronting the unconscious and the equally monumental task of pursuing a profession and maintaining relationships with other human beings at the same time. (Ordinarily this kind of inward turning does not take place and should not take place until one has anchored one's life in reality. I have discussed this developmental theory at some length in Chapter V of *Discernment, A Study in Ecstasy and Evil.*) My friend brought himself out of the confusion by recording faithfully what he had experienced. He wrote his experiences in story form. Still the darkness came back again and again in waves. I noted that each of his stories ended in tragedy, and I suggested to him that until he brought a story around to a positive, creative solution, he would not be able to realize such a condition in actuality in his own life. He nudged his stories to positive conclusions and his life began to mend.

Life does not bring one inevitably toward the light. Without our conscious decision to move toward light and love, our road usually leads downward into the pit. This truth is described in the story of the fall and in the doctrine of original sin. Something within us needs to seek for light and love if they are to be found.

Some people find that they cannot do this kind of fantasy at a typewriter or with a pencil in hand. They have to do it in the wilderness, sitting on a rock or looking out over a wooded valley. I find that a pencil or a typewriter actually stimulates the images, and they begin to come so rapidly that I can hardly keep up with them. Nonetheless it is important to record such experiences when they have occurred without this stimulation. Writing them down gives them concreteness. Looking at what one has written in black and white gives it body and reality.

Also one usually finds that after one has finished, the mood has changed. Things are different inwardly and outwardly. One can record these changes along with the fantasy. When one returns to the experience in the journal, one can relive it and know its reality. This is particularly helpful when the dark voices whisper that one has never been helped and there is no help. *Without a journal in which to record such fantasies and victories, one seldom realizes the potential victory which can be experienced by ordinary human beings like you and me.*

There are times when the darkness is so pervasive and overwhelming that one can hardly function at all. It is then that one needs someone who has been through the darkness and found victory. And one needs to seek and seek until one finds someone to help. In my worst darkness I was shown the way through my inner chaos by one who had escaped from a Nazi concentration camp. A *shaman* is one who has known the darkness of dismemberment and survived and who now helps others toward victory. The church needs people who have dealt with their own inner darkness and survived and come to victory, persons who are available to men and women in this age of anxiety and depression. Only people who have passed through darkness successfully can help others through it. This is the real task of spiritual direction. There is nothing Christianity needs more today than men and women trained as spiritual directors.

Some secular psychologists know something of the inner workings of the human soul. Some Christians know that victory and hope and rebirth are possible as one is committed to Christ. When one is in the worst of darkness one needs both of these abilities fused in one person. If one calls for help to God like the importunate widow, one can usually find such a person even in our time. There is no greater ministry than seeking out the millions of lost and confused people in our world and offering them the way of growth and transformation in Christ. Preaching and intellectual commitment are not enough. Modern men and women need spiritual direction. Journals are the sacrament of spiritual guidance.

Moods and emotions

Emotions and moods come in a thousand different shapes and sizes. Indeed, every inner emotional state is unique, has its own distinctive quality, and its own specific "outpicturing." For nearly 30 years I have been working with my inner being through imagination. I have discovered that each time I turn inward to deal with my inner being a new picture arises, a new story unfolds.

There are many different emotions which can be turned into images. However, one can distinguish a dozen or so different emotions. They are like the more common colors from which all the other colors can be obtained. Let us take a look at some of these more common emotions.

First of all there are anger and fear. These two emotions have a similar physiological reaction. Both are responses to threat and hurt. One is the fight response and the other the flight response. Both require great expenditure of energy.

Fear robs life of value and separates one from God. Constant fear can gradually develop into a chronic anxiety state. Everything becomes fearful. When the phone rings, I wonder who is after me now. God's loving care seems a million miles away. I know of no other way to transform this state of fear except by turning the mood into images of it and bringing Christ into the scene to deal with the fear and heal the hurt.

Much of the tragedy in the world is caused by anger. Because people are hurt they strike out at the world. Not even knowing what it is that makes them so angry, they strike out at anything or anybody that gets in their way. It is difficult to imagine the rage that boils in many people. The tragedy about anger is that it seldom brings about a creative solution. When anger strikes at another it usually calls forth a similar response. Continued anger and retaliation lead to tragedy. One current fad among marriage counselors is to teach people how they can fight fairly. This is better than warfare. However, true intimacy is seldom achieved by fair fighting, as Luciano L'Abate of Georgia State University has shown. Intimacy between people is more likely to be found as people see the hurts lurking within their angers and share these hurt feelings with one another.

If I am to deal with anger rather than having it deal with me, I first of all need to face the fact that the anger is within me, and then I need to record it in my journal. I must realize that venting it on others usually hurts them and seldom accomplishes anything creative. As I reflect on those who have caused me harm I often realize that they have been misshapen and deformed by life. Often they were so unconscious that they truly could not help doing what they did. What then can I do with my anger?

I can turn my anger on God, who has created this world. He did not create evil, but at least he has allowed the horrible evil which so often engulfs us. Indeed, the almighty Father is the only one on whom I can vent my wrath and be sure that I will do no harm. Often pious Christians are afraid to turn to God and express their anger. They fear they will be zapped. This is certainly not seeing God as the loving, caring Father that he is. If I sat by the pool in Phoenix and listened to my 19-year-old son tell me that he never liked me very well, I am sure that God, who is infinitely more loving than I, can take such treatment. My listening to my son express his feelings of rejection and anger has opened us up to a new possibility of relationship which has since flowered into a magnificent friendship.

Many years ago I remember telling God how angry I was that I had to suffer all the pain and confusion which I was experiencing. I told him what I thought of him and his universe with all of its misery and pain and suffering. I wrote out all the anger, bitterness, hostility, hatred, and fury that were in me. When I was finished it was as if there was a presence which was chuckling and a voice which said to me: "Are you finished now, little one? Is there anything else you want to say? I know that you hurt and I am glad that you can express the hurt and anger. I know what you experience, for men and women nailed me to a cross. Come, I understand." I then felt a warmth and a presence and the anger dissipated. I saw things in a different perspective. I was able to go on without being blinded and crippled by my anger. Once when I was angry and asked God why he did not destroy all the evil in the world, all the works of the evil one, he replied that he would have to destroy all human beings to do that, and he loved them and did not want to destroy them.

In the Book of Job we find Job crying out to God in anger and pain. God seems to like that kind of honesty better than pretending love for him when we are raging inside. He would rather have us take our anger out on him rather than letting it out on human beings. The warfare which tears apart human society and destroys millions is often the result of our repressed hostility let out in social destruction. How much better to cry out to God as Jung did in his difficult and often misunderstood book, *The Answer to Job* (Princeton, 1972). That book is a meditation which Jung wrote as he was recovering from a painful and nearly fatal illness. A Lutheran minister in one of my classes remarked that Jung's relationship with God in that book was much more real than most pious theological discussions he had read. In his anger Jung was talking to a real God. The only ultimate cure for our angers and fears is to find a loving center at the heart of being which binds up our hurts and gives peace and joy.

Depression

In depression life seems valueless and tasteless or worse. Someone recently quipped that we have moved from an age of anxiety to an age of depression. In depression there seems no way out. There is a dark voice which suggests that we simply do away with ourselves and rid the earth of the excrement of our presence. Suicide is the ultimate expression of depression, its nadir. When anger and fear no longer divert us from the depth of our hurt, then like a fog rolling in from the ocean comes the gray blanket of depression. Nothing separates us more completely from God than this sense of lostness and despair.

There are four essentially different kinds of depression. There is depression which is legitimate. Our beloved are sick or have died, our friends have betrayed us, or disaster has struck in some material way. Only the insensitive person does not feel depressed when life caves in. Writing out the causes of natural depression and seeing them in the perspective of eternity often helps sustain one until time heals. A second kind of depression is anger turned against one's self. Sometimes when we are burning with anger and cannot let it out on God or any human being, we turn this anger against ourselves and experience it as hopelessness and depression. One deals with this depression by facing the hurt and rage associated with it and bringing it before God as we have already suggested. There are also some depressions which are physiologically induced. After flu and certain other diseases, a feeling of lassitude and heaviness may descend on us. Low blood sugar and certain other physiological imbalances can also contribute to depression.

And last of all there is simple depression, depression which is the common cold of modern psychiatry. (Manic-depressive psychosis is quite a different problem. In this sickness moods of depression alternate with times of elation. This condition can often be controlled by medication.) Many people look out into a meaningless world in which there is no afterlife, where all their projects are doomed to extinction, where all relationships end in death, where sudden death may strike at any moment, and faithfulness is a rare quality. . . . The person who does not feel depressed under such circumstances is not very bright. *Depression is normal and natural in a meaningless world.* Mood elevators or tranquilizers only lead further down the path of absurdity. For such depression there is only one cure—finding a center of powerful, meaningful love at the center of the universe.

In order to experience that kind of meaning, one needs first of all to face the depth of depression in which one finds oneself. One cannot truly seek or find meaning until one realizes that one does not have it. Then one steps into the darkness with courage and with hope of finding meaning on the other side. Finally one seizes the light and hangs on to it until one comes to know the reality of light and love. This process is very nearly impossible without the use of a journal. Few people will bother to use this process of transformation unless they are already keeping a journal. The meditation found earlier in this chapter illustrates these three steps in overcoming depression.

Guilt is a strange combination of fear, depression, and anger. At bottom those who are overwhelmed by guilt have never truly accepted the reality of a loving, forgiving God. They still fear judgment and condemnation. Until they bring all of themselves to the loving God and find that all of one can be forgiven and redeemed there will continue to be guilt. Often we are angry, depressed, and guilty because we have not worked harder at achieving our potential. Some people set themselves such impossible standards of perfection that they are doomed to hopelessness and de-

pression. The actual loving God never expects from us
more than we can attain. We are often more demanding
of ourselves than God.

In *The Other Side of Silence* I have given many examples of dealing with depression in this way. They were not
written for publication, but to deal with my own doubt,
depression, and meaninglessness. I have received many letters of gratitude for sharing those meditations. Within a few
hours of writing "Three Violent Meditations" and "I Met
Death Face to Face," the moods which occasioned these
writings lifted and I experienced the love of God again.

When men and women are still imbedded within a culture or subculture which believes the Christian gospel, the
sacraments of the church can effectively minister to these
moods which we have been describing. Jung has called the
Christian dogmatic system the most effective program of
mental health known to humankind. Fortunate are those
who can be ministered to in this way. However, many modern men and women live and work in an unbelieving world.
They are infected by it. Most of them must find an individual, one-to-one contact with the loving God if they are
going to be rescued from the hopelessness which is endemic
in Western civilization.

Other emotions and moods

There are many other emotions which can be understood
within silence and worked through in journal writing.
First there is the complex of emotions centering around egotism. When one does not have a God, one must become
unified in oneself, and this causes considerable pressure for
ordinary human beings. Behind most stress and tension is

the fear that one must run one's life without help. If all good things must be obtained in this life, to be enjoyed now, then there is the mad scramble to achieve them right away. Discouragement is often little more than disillusioned egotism.

If all joy and satisfaction must be obtained in this life, then the desire for things, for material possessions and pleasures, can become an obsession. Sexual desire, one of the most intense human pleasures, can possess men and women so they are no longer free. These desires can become insatiable. One of the best ways of dealing with these things is to take one's journal and spend some time in reflection and quietness, seeking to penetrate the meaning of these compulsive desires and obtain an external objectivity which puts them in their proper perspective. One can let these emotions take form in images and then bring Christ in to show how they can be handled. Human possessions and sexuality are not evil in themselves, but become evil when they possess us. Within the confidentiality of a journal they can be examined and given a proper place in our lives.

Christianity is the only religion on the face of the earth which takes evil and its manifestations seriously and offers a solution to overcome them. The cross and death of Christ tell us loud and clear that the reality of the universe knows the pain and agony of human suffering. The resurrection reminds us that there is a solution to evil. Bringing one's sickness and physical pain to the loving God is the only way I know to help suffering human beings in distress. One can bear this pain if it does not seem to be in vain. And for those in psychic pain there is great comfort in Jesus' cry on the cross, *"Eloi, Eloi, lama sabachthani"* (Mark 15:34). This kind of pain without hope leads downward toward depression. When one has penetrated through this pain and found light on the other side, it is helpful to write down what one has experienced. Such writing actualizes the victory. Later on in times of difficulty one can turn back to what has been written, and this gives ground to stand on in dealing with inner and outer pain.

I wrote the following words in my journal as I was dealing with the pain of some friends. Their pain left its mark on my inner being.

What heals the deep, deep hurt, the nearly mortal wound?
What mends the broken heart, allowing it to beat
Again, and force the blood in limbs and hands and head?
What brings the brutal pain of sap flowing in the frozen tree?
The buds are bursting forth with flowers soon to come.
Then seeds which die to rise once more and so
The agony continues on. What balm can heal
The deep, deep hurt? The answer is too trite, so known
And yet unknown or yet unlived, misunderstood.
Is it not love, real caring which expects no gift,
No recompense, not even one kind word?
The energy which drives the planets and the stars,
The care, the basic stuff which gives all motion, form
And life. The love unveiled on cross at Calvary,
This love which made the heart alone can heal
The deep, deep hurt of life and staunch the flow
Of poison oozing from the wounded earth, so torn
And bleeding and yet so afraid it might be cured.
Oh come, oh loving light and heal the deep dark wound
Within my breast and bubble forth a spring to quench
The burning thirst we humans have for more than peace,
Release from pain and fear. Please use my stinking wound
To comfort me and others now, to bring us to Abba,
My father, friend, who heals the deep, deep wound
And so reveals to us the Lover, divine and prodigal.

And then there is the pain of loneliness and boredom, feeling separated and cut off from other human beings and from any meaning. The person who is bored with life finds every action an effort; every day is the same meaningless routine. The person who cannot use the imagination to penetrate into the heart of these conditions and use them as a way of finding the victorious, loving God is greatly impoverished. Indeed I know of no other solution to these destructive emotions than to penetrate through them and to encounter the loving Christ who is to be found within and beyond our inner confusion and pain.

When the church is truly the church it will minister to the loneliness of human beings. In our atomized and fragmented society people can easily become lost and lonely. James Lynch has shown conclusively the destructive effect of loneliness in his book *The Broken Heart*. Loneliness destroys the bodies as well as the souls of human beings. The church needs to provide fellowship as well as meaning for those who are lonely. Preaching love without extending it to the needy borders on hypocrisy.

Actualizing the positive emotions

There are times when our hearts sing with joy. Life appears beautiful, and everything falls in place. We have a sense of being loved, and we are carried to the seventh or tenth heaven. These moods and emotions may come after a time of testing and trial or they may come out of the blue and fill life with radiant meaning. We know for the moment that behind the physical world lies a spiritual one that is characterized by love, and we are lifted into the midst of that meaning. It is important to record one's moments of ecstasy if one would knit them into the fabric of one's existence and build one's life around them. It is as important to record and concretize one's significant religious experiences as it is to avoid and work through negative moods and emotions.

All great religious poetry is an expression of this kind of experience. Dante's *Divine Comedy* was written during a period when Dante was banished from his beloved city of Florence and living from hand to mouth. This story-poem starts in a dark wood, leads one through hell and purgatory, ending in a vision of heaven described in these words:

> High phantasy lost power and here broke off;
> Yet, as a wheel moves smoothly, free from jars,
>   My will and my desire were turned by love,
> The love that moves the sun and the other stars.

Helen Luke has provided a magnificent understanding of *The Divine Comedy* in her book, *Dark Wood to White Rose* (Dove, 1975). Here is religious imagination and poetry at its greatest.

The poetry of St. John of the Cross expresses the same experience of being touched and transformed by the love of the risen Christ. One of the most impressive descriptions of St. John's experience is found in the poem entitled, *The Dark Night,* or "Song of the soul in rapture at having arrived at the height of perfection, in which is union with God by the road of spiritual negation":

> Oh night that was my guide!
> Oh darkness dearer than the morning's pride,
> Oh night that joined the lover
> To the beloved bride
> Transfiguring them each into the other.

> Within my flowering breast
> Which only for himself entire I save
> He sank into his rest

And all my gifts I gave
Lulled by the airs with which the cedars wave.

Over the ramparts fanned
While the fresh wind was fluttering his tresses,
With his serenest hand
My neck he wounded, and
Suspended every sense with its caresses.

Lost to myself I stayed
My face upon my lover having laid
From all endeavour ceasing;
And all my cares releasing
Threw them amongst the lilies there to fade.

(St. John of the Cross, Poems, with a translation by Roy Campbell (Penguin, 1968), pp. 28-29. There is no finer collection of great mystical poetry than these poems of St. John of the Cross. The Spanish text is provided along with a fine English translation.)

Expressing one's joy gives substance to the spiritual life. One can write a story, do a dance, run along the beach as the sun is setting, paint a picture or write a poem. It is very helpful to make a record of these experiences. Few people do this unless they have a journal at hand to write in.

I wrote the following words after an experience of the love of God. Writing these words made the experience much more real. Anyone can let the words and images pour out of one's deepest self.

Timberline revisited

The golden hours have come and gone
The golden dew has fallen once again.
Has growth occurred, change towards maturity?
A new level? A new place?
A sudden sunny day, the glory once the storm is past.

I remember the glory of a day now past.
The best of that was gathered up and sanctified.

The tree at timberline still stands,
In spite of violent wind and raging snow,
The sleet and ice and sheets of rain,
Torrents as the skies broke open, the deluge
Humans feared so long, perhaps.
These broke upon the tree relentlessly
As waves against a rocky shore.
And yet the twisted pine still stands,
The seed cones clinging to its limbs
Ready to hurl infinite life into the storm
And spread its potential upon the wreckage,
The debris, the chaos left behind.

The tree remembers as only the rugged can
A fall of golden pollen, heavenly dew.
The memory breaks the seal of fate
And brings the sudden sunny day
And with it another curious seeker
Who scales the cliffs and rests his naked back
Against the knotted bark and gazes out
Upon horizons limitless, range on range
Of mountains, valleys, peaks, ridges
Stretching out until the eye is tired,
Drugged with so much grandeur.
Only sleep can rest the ecstasy.
And then a greater glory stirs both
The tree and youth—a sinking sun
Runs riot through the skies and paints
With colors, hues, no palette ever held—
Salmon, rose, ruby red and pink.
All blending in a golden haze, pulsing
With the dance, but now to steps
Of glory, not of pain or hurt,
Of wind or hail. Now a playground
Of joyous colors where the dazzling tints

Are dancing now a polka, now a minuet.
Each delicate hue alive with love,
Expressing love, harmony, bliss, delight,
The love which drops the sun beneath
The furthest range and sings as she daubs
The skies in brilliant poetry of sight.

There is something new to remember
Even better than the golden dew.
The conjunction is complete and slowly
Falls the night in a peal of wine-dark royal purple.
The youth draws his cloak about him and watches
As the stars spring one by one from the sea-like heaven
Like flying fish, those stars also moved by love.
He will remember this spot and come again.
He sleeps and dreams of lovers he won't forget,
Of visions when the heavens opened—
Of Him, divine lover, who brought about
The perfect conjunction and keeps alive its reality
Until the time of fulfillment comes again.
No storm is needed now, only the right elements and time.
The dream is more real than waking life,
Revealing Him from whom the glory streams.

Imagination as the gateway inward

When we are quiet and turn inward we can usually begin
to observe images which arise from the depth of our beings.
It is as if we have dipped down into the level of life from
which dreams spring forth. The images and stories which
spring up from this level reveal a great deal about our
inner lives. They show us as we are in the bedrock of our
lives. Often we find things which we do not like, things
which need to be changed. We can find lust, anger, vio-
lence, destructiveness, and lostness which we did not know
were within us. Some of us have such solid ego structures

that these things do not press up toward consciousness in moods and emotions, but are only revealed in the fantasy which quietness releases.

There are many different ways in which we can touch this level of ourselves. The first way is meditative silence. We are quiet until the images begin to bubble forth, and then we follow where they lead. Or we can start with dreams that are meaningful. Many years ago I had a dream of being at an ocean beach. A large turtle came up out of the water and began talking to me. When I awakened I could not remember what the turtle had said, and I felt cheated. I decided to see if I could return to the dream in my imagination. A day or so later I became quiet and imagined that I was in the dream scene at the beach once again. The turtle came up out of the water. This time it would not talk to me, but instead went to a rocky cliff behind me and tapped three times on it. A doorway opened in the cliff, and I went in to discover a whole new dimension of reality. Each month for two years I returned to the imaginative story and let it continue. Eighty thousand words later the saga came to an end. I found within me a hundred of the myths of humankind springing spontaneously from the depths of me and tailored to fit my present condition. I learned much about myself and was able to make some very significant changes in my life.

There are many ways of stimulating this imaginative process. In the Thematic Apperception Test (TAT), subjects are shown pictures which could have different meanings. They are then asked to tell stories involving these pictures. It is startling to see how much of an individual is revealed in his or her stories.

One cannot tell a story without revealing something about

one's self. Robert Louis Stevenson's story, *Dr. Jekyll and Mr. Hyde,* revealed the split not only in Stevenson, but in Victorian England as well. Emily Bronte's *Wuthering Heights* portrayed her own destructive animus. Shakespeare could only bring resolution to his tragedies in his last three plays when some resolutions had been made in his own life. Most fiction springs out of the depths of an individual and reveals the inner life, the problems and struggles of the one who tells the tale.

Asking people to write their own fairy tales can stimulate their imagination so that the depths of individuals are revealed. Likewise asking someone to draw an island or a person will reveal the inner attitudes of that individual. A young man came to see me many years ago. He felt that his dreams were too pedestrian and revealing, and so instead of telling me his dreams he made up truly magnificent mythical stories. He related these to me as if they were his dreams. He did not realize that he was revealing his inmost being just as effectively as if he had told me his dreams.

Another young man, a professional counselor, used the same process of storytelling consciously with powerful effect. He found that active imagination as we have described it did not produce the desired results. His dream life did not give him the guidance which he needed and so he wrote stories which brought him into touch quite consciously with the depth of his unconscious and enabled him to deal very creatively with the contents which he discovered there. Indeed I know of no better example of the use of a story for self-discovery and transformation than the following story which Dr. Douglas Daher has given me permission to reproduce in full.

One afternoon in the middle of time, on the edge of space, upon the earth's mass and with a burst of energy, four children came out to play. The day was October 31 and for this Halloween the children had specific plans. There was a forest on the other side of the lake that none of the four had ever visited, until today. For most of the summer they had been building a raft which would carry them across the water to the mysterious woods. Seth, the most courageous boy for miles around, had first conceived the plan and convinced the others not to be afraid of such adventure. Peggy, the real brain of the four, used her unusual intelligence to conceive and draft prints of what type of raft would be needed to cross the rather large and unpredictable lake. As for the actual construction of the raft, Mark had the best pair of hands that had been seen for a long time in those parts. He was a genuine maker. And finally, there was Dorothy, whose particular gift was her constant kindness to those around her. Dorothy provided the support and encouragement when the other three might have given up.

Today was the day to launch the raft toward the forest beyond. How well their talents had blended to bring them to the possibility of such an adventure. The long process and complicated task of building a large and sturdy raft had strengthened the already close bonds of friendship between the four. However, despite the months of communal efforts, neither Seth nor Peg, neither Mark nor Dorothy dared to share with each other their secret shames. Perhaps each was afraid the others would not understand; perhaps each one was too distracted with their promise of adventure; perhaps there was not time; for whatever reason, the secret shames lay hidden within.

All was ready by late afternoon for launching. Seth, serving as the commander, gave the word to be pushed off, and so the foursome were on their way. Peg had conceived an emblem that Mark reproduced upon the flag—an eagle with a proud, independent, self-sufficient stance. Dorothy had made plenty of chocolate chip cookies in case of a shipwreck. How excited were the faces of the children as the raft drifted out over the lake.

The depth and darkness of the waters below did not concern them.

The lake was particularly calm, so the children found the paddling not very difficult, but the distance to the forest was far. Not until dark, with the moon already announcing her reign, did the raft arrive on the bank which threaded between the water and trees. Upon landing, Mark made sure the raft was well secured as Seth already was scouting with his eyes where they should enter the forest. Sought-for adventures seem to have a point of stillness, when the beginning is at hand. At such time, doubts play their game of be afraid until the talents, which begin such quests, rally and shoo them away. Into the woods the young ones went.

They had not traveled long before the sun was completely down and only fractures of the moon rays reached through the trees. Deciding to rest under an oak, the four barely had found places to sit when a shrieking laugh sprung them to their feet. Suddenly before them was an ugly, fat, wrinkled-skin hag. "Ya ha ha ha," she shrieked again as one of her withered hands reached toward them. "So, you come into our woods to give yourselves as gifts, so very nice presents to have," the hag laughed as the four kids were stuck in their fright and dread. The hag was delighted to find four darling and pretty children to possess. Seth, despite his courage, could not move to defend them against the hag. Peg had no ideas and Mark no weapons to use. Only Dorothy heard an inner voice that provided a choice. "That is you, Dorothy, in part and unless you claim her as your own, she will carry all of you away into the shadows." Dorothy was face-to-face with her secret shame. A secret for her it could remain but the power of the hag was upon them. In a choice fairly remarkable for one so young, Dorothy stepped forward, gently clasped the withered hand and turned to her friends saying, "I want you to meet my friend, the envious hag." To the utter surprise of the other three kids the hag gratefully accepted Dorothy's acknowledgement of her and clearly stepped back to let Dorothy take over. Dorothy could have at that point gone into a long explanation of how well she knew this envious hag, the many occasions she had fought with her and waved her off to leave her alone; but instead she simply told her companions that the hag was a secret friend and would not harm them now that Dorothy was not ashamed. The other three were greatly relieved, but not entirely pleased when Dorothy invited the hag to accompany them. The hag readily accepted and the five walked further into the moonlit darkness.

After such an unexpected and shocking event, it would be only fair that we are allowed some rest, thought Seth; but never let it be said that the forest is just and fair. They had barely walked five minutes before they arrived at the keenest tree fort one could ever imagine. The platforms, ladders, windows, and trap doors all were constructed with such skill and precision. So inviting was this fort of forts that the kids climbed up into it without a second thought, but the hag simply sat below to wait. The four had not even time for an ounce of fun when out of a secret closet stepped a large and mean troll. If a hag freezes one in fear, a troll sends such tremors through one's limbs that one can barely stand. "So you have come to use and steal my fort. How dare you touch what I work so hard to make," growled the troll. Seth wanted to bravely respond about their intentions, but only stammered. Peg thought she understood well what was happening but had no vision as to what to do. Dorothy was about to be kind, but it was obvious that the troll was not at all interested in such gestures. But Mark, yes Mark, knew what the troll was going to say even before he said it. How often Mark had inwardly heard such complaints and pretended he didn't hear. As Mark pondered about his knowing him well, the troll was opening the jail cell of the fort that was equipped with all sorts of finely made torture devices. Dorothy noticed that Mark was unusually pensive and gave him a not so gentle nudge to do something. Mark took a deep breath, walked right up to the troll and shook his hand vigorously. "I have heard you've been trying to meet me for a long time," Mark said, "but I haven't been around." When the troll frowned in disbelief, Mark added, "I mean, I've told you I haven't been in to keep you away.

Now, I want to meet you and perhaps I can be a little less put off by your selfishness." That seemed to satisfy the troll and he began to take Mark on a personal tour of the fort with the others close behind. As Dorothy had done with the hag, Mark invited the troll to join them. Peg was not entirely comfortable with the thought of this new companion, Seth figured he would more than pull his weight in case of a battle, and Dorothy was surprised that she was pleased to have the troll come along, since he was now Mark's secret friend.

Off again the children went, being a party of six. They had no idea of the time, but the moon was full overhead. After what seemed a rather long walk they approached a clearing where the moonlight shown through directly. Into the middle of the clearing Seth led the three kids, having the strange sensation that he was walking onto a stage which was lit by a huge spotlight. The hag and troll waited in the shadows. Dorothy and Mark were still not well practiced in keeping tabs on their new friends. Then began the echoes almost before the howl—a wolf was upon them. To be shocked and frightened by ugly or large human forms is one matter, but to be matched against one of nature's primitive animals is quite another fright. The wolf was slinking around growling at each as he sniffed them. Yet, another shock in the midst of their almost petrified states, the wolf could talk! No mere animal, he was a werewolf.

"I command these woods and do not recall any of you requesting my permission to come here. I like adventures, though, especially ones that feed me," chuckled the werewolf. His mouth was watering as he ground his teeth a bit and then pranced in proud delight to have such game. Peg, Mark and Dorothy were truly too frightened to be aware of any of their intuitive whispers. Seth, the boy of such courage, was not so out of sorts. For as the wolf pranced in his taunting delight at his own cleverness, Seth recognized the dance as one his own shadow would perform when he was brave. This man-turned-wolf under the spotlight of the moon was none other than his own fierce pet, whom he seldom cared for and never spoke of to others. If Seth ever had a desire to flee it was now, to escape the jaws of this nasty creature. Perhaps if the wolf devoured his friends first, he might have a chance. The most courageous boy in the land did not flee, but met the proud beast eye to teeth. Seth marched over and wrapped his arm around the neck of the animal in an affectionate hug as one does with a beautiful collie. No more was needed for the animal to sit and lap his companion's hand with his tongue.

Enough adventure for one Halloween, was the consensus of the group of seven as they wound their way back toward the raft. "Hags, trolls, werewolves," thought Peg, "I never imagined such creatures in my thoughts let alone in my life." The other three children walked silently but each paying needed attention to their own new friend. Upon reaching the raft and much to their surprise, they were greeted by a tall slender woman dressed in shades of gray. She was sweeping their raft with her broom. None of them were frightened by her, quite to the contrary, she spoke to them in such a clear and profound speech that they became quite unconcerned by her presence. The more Seth, Mark and Dorothy asked the woman questions, the more they were intrigued by her cleverness. Only Peg refrained from talking to the gray draped figure, for she knew all too well that she was a sorceress. Could her companions not see that in all her attentiveness to their questions she was quite indifferent to them, their needs and their safety? No, of course the others couldn't, for the witch's manner of apathy was quite unfamiliar to them. Peg had often glimpsed this cold-hearted woman flying in and out of her world of ideas, but never found her interesting enough to pay attention to. Now the witch was mesmerizing her companions by clever but empty verse because it lacked caring. Without a flinch of fear, her companions didn't realize that this encounter with the sorceress was probably their most dangerous adventure so far. For if the spell she was casting was not shattered, the group might stay there forever, or at least a very long time, on a shore away from home. How revealing it would be for her to approach the witch and name the spell. The others would never guess her knowing if she chose not to do so, of that Peg was sure. Intelligence is not always a foe of wisdom; Peg approached the sorceress with knowing eyes. "Long have I waited to meet you," the gray flanked woman gracefully responded to the girl's advance. "Too long have I had you wait," Peg replied. The woman and girl embraced and with such contact the others seemed to awaken from a haze. Seth proclaimed, "Onto the raft for our return." The darkness of Halloween night still persisted.

The children and their four secret companions were truly a sight as they crossed the lake once again. The range of their talents was impressive and the strength of their numbers apparent. What adventures for a Halloween night, and happily they floated over the depthful water on their return.

Only the naive die young. The children were still so unaware of their world.

The mist they floated into seemed unusual for the lake, much denser than any of them could remember ever seeing on the lake. Always before, though, they had stood on the shore, and with the mist came a chill that they knew should not have been there for an October night. This coldness was piercing and cruel, and then the foul stench sucked in the air, choking out any semblance of freshness. Seth whispered to Peg, "What's going on?"

She replied ever so slowly, "I don't think we have ever understood what the darkness can be, I fear the worst."

Tears came to Dorothy's eyes even as the hag held her ever so tight. Mark's glorious hands were knotted, knuckles white. The raft began to swirl. Underneath, far underneath a blackness was emerging to engulf them. Breaking through the water's surface were slimy tentacles which whipped every which way. Sharp and poisonous vines from below struck, struck, struck the children without repose. Then out of the water rose the creature of hate which sliced through life with ease. There was no dialogue with this hideous strength which attacked them. There were no reasons why they were to suffer and die. There was only its domination of their every movement, thought, hope, cries, and tears.

Shredded were the young babes, their raft and secret friends into jagged meaningless parts, but the pain would not end. For as each child was strewn through the foul stench and mist, each child could see, could weep, but for what? The blackness howled without words, and mocked even their lonely remaining souls. Seth, boy of courage, why had you ever believed that your noble deeds would make a difference? Peg, the child of thought, what good is wisdom in my world? Mark, the maker of goods, whose pleasure serves your creations now? And Dorothy, fool of kindness, scorned be you most of all for your impotent gestures of love!

Though no question was asked of that final remaining child's soul, she simply gestured to the horizon one more time as light broke through the darkness. Light, which should have been dim from such a distance, pierced all the life and all the death that was on the lake. He came forth in the lightness and bent and kneeled and wept at the sight He beheld. As His tears dropped to the lake all the foulness was dispersed. With His arms He reached out wide and gathered all the broken parts. One who is all courageous, and suffered Himself among proud men, even forgiving them; this is the One who placed Seth back upon the raft. One whose wisdom grasps all and understands the burdens of knowing too much; this is the One who rolled Peg upon the raft. One who makes all and trusts His creation even to those who might abuse it; this is the One who put Mark upon the raft. One who loves and has such patience with those who are distracted by other gifts; this is the One who gently lifted Dorothy upon the raft.

Dorothy looked forth upon the face that loved her and knew to ask, "Where are our four secret friends. Will they not also be healed and returned?"

"Your secret friends are with you, and closer than ever before, try not to forget them."

Seth stood up and wondered, "Why do you not destroy that blackness forever?"

"If I were to destroy it now, so many caught in its horrid arms would also be lost. Am I to abandon them, or even it? We must wait, but fight the struggle well."

Peg's head was gushing with a myriad of ideas and pondered,

"Where did it ever come from and how does it continue to survive?"

"The where and why you are yet to learn, but I guess now you know that it is fed to survive each time secret shames are left in the depths and abandoned. Your shames were saved, partly by their persistence of you to befriend them, many are not."

Finally, after a short time, Mark stood, bowed, and offered in his cupped hand a stick, man-made from the stiff grass that bound the raft.

"Creation needs more who are willing to make man in his divine image."

Morning was upon them and the raft approached the shore of home. The four children did not, as in each year past, regret the passing of Halloween.

To the bank they waded in, pulling the raft aground. Smiles upon their faces, hands grasped, they had returned on this November 1, All Saints' Day.

Stepping imaginatively into the Bible

There are few people who are not touched by a good story. We get caught up by a meaningful tale and actually step into the inner reality of the person who tells it. There is a mystery in storytelling which plumbs the depth of the human soul. Myths and fairy tales express the common psychic depths of a group of people. When we listen to them we are touched and changed by the meanings which the stories express. We enter a common inner world and perceive an inner road map laid out before us. We see the grain of that reality and know what things go against that grain and what things go with it.

C. S. Lewis once described myth as a pattern of reality which can be expressed either in imagination or in history. Christians need not be disturbed by the story of the Hindu god Ganesha who died and rose again or tales of the many dying and rising gods of Asia Minor in the centuries before Christ. These people had perceived imaginatively an aspect of the nature of spiritual reality which was later written into the fabric of history in the death and resurrection of Jesus of Nazareth. The entire Bible narrative moves inexorably toward the revelation of the love of God which is revealed in the triumphant victory of Jesus over death and evil.

It is one thing to know this victory intellectually and another to let that victory move and shape one's entire being. How does one allow the reality of victorious love to shape the course and substance of one's life and to transform one's inner being? How can one appropriate the love, hope, courage, humility, joy, and faith which sing through the gospel narratives? How does one allow the Holy Spirit to move in and through one's life and renew and shape it?

One important way to know this new life is to step imaginatively into the biblical narratives. The real purpose of Bible reading is not just to learn facts and figures, but to be transformed by sharing in its stories and life. I have a friend who decided that as an educated man he should read and know the New Testament. He was very bright, and so he remembered every story and fact, but it did him little good. He was outside the movement of the story. He did not participate in its myth, in its meaning, in its life. He might just as well have read the *Wall Street Journal*.

Walter Wink has suggested that much modern, historical, biblical criticism has lost its purpose and become bankrupt. The purpose of studying the Bible is not to write scholarly papers for other scholars, but to step into its life and find transformation. He states this point of view clearly and well in his book *The Bible in Human Transformation* (Fortress,

1973). He does use biblical criticism and historical research about biblical times and customs, but his central focus is on revealing the radical nature of the biblical narrative so that people can come more easily to its transforming power.

Dryden Phelps and L. Earl Willmott have provided an excellent guide for those who would study the Bible in this manner in *Exploring the Mind of Jesus* (Friendship, 1974). This book provides practical, concrete ways for getting into the biblical story so that it may be a leaven to permeate all of one's life, conscious and unconscious. Dr. Reneta Glass, one of my former students, is at present working on a book dealing with the mystery of story and its theological significance. The importance of the Bible's stories for constant transformation and renewal of human beings can hardly be overemphasized.

When we are truly living within the framework and meaning of the Christian story, many changes take place. First of all we look at all of life from the perspective of eternity. Our essential meaning is given by a loving God who dwells beyond time and space as well as within this physical world. The evil and difficulties of life are not of God. They come from the evil one, and he has been defeated. This world is important, and we show the authenticity of our following Christ more by our love for one another than in any other way. We know that we move toward an eternal, resurrected, immortal life which surpasses anything that we can imagine or hope for.

We can appropriate the reality which the Christian story reveals. We can incorporate this reality not only into our thinking, feeling, and acting, but can even allow it to transform our emotions. Most of the negative moods which I have described earlier in this chapter lose their power when the Christian story is truly taken up into our lives. Fear, anger, depression, tension, and guilt can be kept at arm's length. Even our desire for things and our sexual desires can be transformed and transmuted into caring, self-giving love. This does not happen by chance, but only as I nurture that reality within my life.

Let me repeat that no other religious story offers the same transforming power. Most of Islam presents a vision of a god before whom we tremble, a god more characterized by oriental authority and omnipotence than love and friendship. Buddha tells us that the world is irredeemable and that all emotions —love included—are to be annihilated. Only Christianity offers transformation into the fullness of the stature of Christ.

In medieval times, when few people could read and write, monks came to church services frequently to praise God and share in the inner meaning of the Bible's story. First of all a narrative was read (the *lectio*). Then time was given to think about the story and its meaning (the *meditatio*). Then one stepped into its meaning and encountered the divine reality which the story expressed (the *contemplatio*). Real Bible reading requires all three of these processes.

A journal can be an important aid in recording the insights and experiences one has in stepping into the life of the Bible's story. What is only thought about and not recorded in word or drawing is seldom fully incorporated into one's life.

For thirty years it was necessary as the pastor of a church to produce a sermon weekly. When I finally learned the secret of stepping into Bible narratives I found that sermons were easy to write. I simply shared on Sunday morning my meditative journeys into Scripture. Those imaginative trips, which spoke to my inner condition and brought healing to me, also often brought meaning and hope to others. I am grateful for the necessity which forced me to do this kind of work.

One need never fear entering the Bible, as it *always* leads one toward transformation and renewal. I have shared some of these imaginative journeys into the Bible in "Windows Inward," the last section of *The Other Side of Silence*. In these stories I imagine myself with Mary on the road to Bethlehem where she is to give birth to the Christ child, and I realize how difficult it is to allow the Christ child to be born into one's life. Or I see myself with the other Mary at the open tomb and weep with her until the Lord calls her name and mine and our sorrow is banished. I walk with Jesus as he raises Lazarus from the stench of death and decomposition and realize that he can transform and redeem anything in me. I help carry a paralytic to Jesus and let him down through the roof and realize that Jesus can heal my inner and outer crippledness as well.

In two books I have entered into the reality of the crucifixion and the resurrection through imagination. In *The Hinge* (Religious Publ., 1977) I find myself at the crucifixion and see seven people transformed by Jesus' last words on the cross. In *The Age of Miracles* (Ave Maria, 1979) I imagine seven people coming into a church and finding renewal as they live through the victory of Jesus on Calvary.

Anyone can do this kind of imaginative sortie in the spiritual reality of the Bible. First of all it is important to see its value and take the time. I know of no better way of appropriating the victory of the good news. A woman from South Carolina attended a conference in which I suggested biblical exploration of this kind. She tried it and found it opened the Scriptures to her. As this happened she realized that she had something to say, and began to write a newspaper column. She wrote about how her gifts had been multiplied as she meditated on the story of the feeding of the 5000. She imagined that she was with the little boy who decided that he would go and listen to Jesus on a sunny spring day. He was a very normal little boy, and so he packed a substantial lunch for himself: several loaves of flat, round bread and some dried fish. He didn't like being hungry, and it was several hours' journey to the hillside where Jesus was to be found. A great crowd had already gathered by the time he got there, but he was small and he wormed his way through the crowd. Finally he came to the very edge of the circle of men who kept the crowd from overwhelming Jesus. How that man talked! It fed his heart and soul and mind. Before the crowd knew it the sun was low in the western sky.

Jesus realized the crowd was hungry and that many of the people might not be able to make it all the way home on empty stomachs. He told his disciples to feed the crowd. They laughed at their Master. One of the big fishermen with rough hands noticed that a young boy had a lunch with him and was half offering his food to the Master. The boy's heart swelled in joy and pain as the big man took his lunch and handed it to the Master. Then he saw his humble lunch of dried bread and fish blessed and broken. And it grew and grew and grew until everyone there was fed. The little boy had all he could eat, even more than if he had kept it for himself. This is what happens so often when one offers one's treasures, one's meager little gifts, to God.

Or one can imagine being a guest at the party which Simon the Pharisee gave for Jesus. Everything went smoothly for awhile. Simon was a little distant and formal, but it was a nice party. The food and wine were good. Then a woman walked brazenly into the room where they were reclining at the dinner table. Women were not allowed to enter the company of men. A decent woman would know this. The whole crowd was shocked and amazed, wondering what would happen next.

The woman walked right over to where Jesus was reclining at the table, eating his supper. She began to cry convulsively, sobbing and weeping. Her tears poured forth, and she bathed his feet with them. The woman kissed his feet and then began to wipe them with her hair. It was an incredible display of emotion, tenderness, gratitude, and bad taste. As if this were not enough, she broke open an alabaster jar and poured perfume over Jesus' feet.

A thousand thoughts went through my head as I watched this scene unfold before me. Who was this woman? How did she have access to this house? Was she mad? Her brazenness terrified me. What would I do if she came to me? How dare she come into the house? What was her relationship with Jesus and Simon?

And then Jesus spoke. He knew what Simon was thinking. He told a story about being forgiven much and little. I began to realize that Jesus was critical of Simon for not having welcomed him, for treating him with cold reserve, with niggardly attention. But this wild woman—he began to praise her in extravagant fashion. He said that her sins, which were many, were forgiven because she loved much. I realized that I had a part of me like Simon, an objective observer, but deep within me was a grateful, extravagant, emotional side. I realized that I could only find life as I allowed my deeper feelings to be expressed, so I could be forgiven like this woman. It was worth even making a fool of myself.

The church year offers another way to get into the Christian story. We are given the seasons of Advent and Lent to prepare for Christmas and Easter. After Easter we have the magnificent season in which we try to realize the resurrection of Christ in our own lives. The purpose of the church year is to lead us back through the Christian story again and again. One friend kept a journal of her Lenten journey several years ago. I have seen few more sensitive and moving records of the inner life. This young woman wrote daily of her journey into her own wilderness, into her own temptations. She wrote out passages of poetry which were particularly meaningful. She illuminated the pages with pictures and drawings in many colors. She reflected on the passages of Scripture which were appointed for that season. One could see the growth taking place before one's very eyes. That journey gave her a foundation to withstand storms which came upon her the next year, storms which might have engulfed her had she not had this foundation.

Still another woman led a group of friends on an Advent journey. She took the group from the Annunciation through the first months at Nazareth to the difficult trip to Bethlehem. She told me how much writing out these thoughts had done for her and how they prepared her to accept the beauty and grandeur of Christmas.

Eucharist as a door inward

There is yet another way in which one can enter this inner world of victory and transformation.

Jesus himself ordained this method. It is the Eucharist. In this service we share Jesus' last supper with him, and then we accompany him in his betrayal, death, and resurrection. The Eucharist is the drama in which we follow the risen Christ and participate in his victory.

The Eucharist is more than an intellectual experience. It is an imaginative and dramatic living with the Christ. We share his very food and life. This service more than any other helps us grow into the fullness of the stature of Christ. It is a service in which we need to share again and again. Plants need constant water and the nutrients from the soil. Human beings need food and exercise and caring if they are to grow to their physical potential. They also need the spiritual food and nourishment which inward turning to Christ provides fully and deeply. My wife and I find that we need not only our own private times of stepping into the Bible, but also need the shared inner journey of the Eucharist. We find the daily Eucharist a way in which we can meet and share our individual journeys.

Seldom do we realize the full reality which the Eucharist reveals unless we record something of the experience which it has provided. Nearly every encounter with the risen Christ is richer when we have paused, given thanks for it, and made some record of its meaning.

Conclusion

There are many different ways of actualizing the victory of Christ in our lives. There are many ways of working through the darkness and difficulties which beset all of us. It is not important which of these we select. The important thing is that we begin to be active Christians who are trying to incorporate and appropriate the immeasurable riches of Christ and the kingdom of heaven. A journal is an aid, a companion, and a guide on this inward journey.

10

The Benefits
of Journal Keeping

M Y JOURNAL HAS BEEN my closest companion for over 30 years, a companion always available and ready to respond. With my journal I could share my deepest and darkest secrets, my fears and pains, my confusions and hopelessness. Having written down these dark things about myself, I began to have the courage to look at myself. My journal has also provided me with a record of my inner life, its revelations, insights, joys, and graces. Seeing these things in black and white has given them substance and reality in my life. I could then build on these things. My journal has given me objectivity and distance so that I could find solid ground, get my bearings, and not be engulfed by the storms which have come again and again in my inner and outer life.

Sitting quietly with my copybook open on my lap, I have often found that my inner ears were unstopped and I could hear voices speaking from another dimension of reality. I could even hear the voice of the divine lover himself. Recording the dreams which have been seeking entrance to my conscious mind and trying to understand them has convinced me more and more of the incredible providence of

God. The persistent and constant knocking upon the doorway of my soul by the dreamer within staggers me when I think about it. The journal has stimulated and prodded me to develop my imagination. Through the imagination I have been led into a deeper and deeper relationship with the divine lover. I have found that this one would have me bring all of myself to him for transformation, and my journal has been an invaluable aid in gathering myself together to make that offering.

A common experience

I have already pointed out that some of the greatest devotional classics of the Christian church are simply the records which men and women have written of their encounters with the other. These works are encouraging to most of us because these journals show the ups and downs of the spiritual life. We see from the struggles of these Christian seekers that any of us can go this inner way. We are all beset by the same fears, temptations, dryness, and problems. One good way to prod oneself into journal keeping is to read the journals of John Wesley, John Woolman, Augustine of Hippo, or some other Christian seeker.

The interest in religious or Christian journal keeping is growing on every side. The Benedictine Abbey at Pecos, New Mexico, is one of the most spiritually alive places I know. Journal keeping is recommended for all those in that community. Father Ray Roh, a member of that community, has published a leaflet on *Keeping a Spiritual Journal*. George Simons has written *Keeping Your Personal Journal* (Paulist, 1978) to show the value of this practice in the growing religious life. Milt Hughes has written a book entitled *Spiritual Journey Notebook* which is published by National Student Ministries in Nashville, Tennessee.

Many people have expressed gratitude to me for urging them to keep a spiritual journal, more often than for any other practice which I have suggested. Dozens of people have told me that the discipline of journal keeping has been most helpful in pursuing and deepening their religious lives. Several of my friends have written me telling how much journal keeping has meant to them. I conclude with three personal statements (almost testimonies) concerning the incredible value which can be received from this practice. These writers present the same theme in different variations.

A journal as a life raft

The first of these accounts is written by a gifted psychologist, writer, and counselor. Over the years he has shared much of his journal with me.

I began keeping a journal about ten years ago. At that point, my life had fallen into a state of "existential disrepair." I had lost my bearings and was unable to get back on course.

Morton suggested that I purchase a journal and that I use it to record dreams, fantasies, poetry, drawings, feelings and anything else that I might wish to include. His suggestion was important to me for many reasons. It provided me a "junkheap"; I could put down whatever inner feelings I wished, socially acceptable or not. It gave me an opportunity to take myself seriously. I gradually discovered that although I constantly worried about myself, I didn't have a very high opinion of myself. Working in my journal also helped me to concretize my inner life, to capture it. Feelings which came and went became part of a permanent record. I found that I didn't have to be controlled by these feelings. I discovered through my journal that within me were many different figures, male and female, human and beast, angel and demon, that I could come to know and through whom I could better know myself. I found too a very negative, destructive reality which seemed hell-bent on destroying me and my relationships with others. At times, this destructiveness was overwhelming and I discovered that by calling on God, on Jesus, on the creative forces, that I need not stand alone and helpless against this fearful reality.

Keeping a journal has broadened my inner and outer horizons. I know now that I am a larger, more complex being than ever I had imagined. I know, too, the infinite complexity of life. This has humbled me for I see now that my feelings of self-importance in the world were misguided; the world can manage perfectly well without me. Realizing that, I have paradoxically found a different sort of importance within myself. The statement of my life has changed from "I am important" to "I am."

Keeping a record of my dreams has had a major impact on me. In looking back over these dreams I have come to see that there is a Person working with me through my dreams who usually has a better understanding of my life than I do. It has been reassuring especially during difficult times to discover this Person working with me through a series of dreams.

It is probably no accident that journal and journey are related words. Writing in one's journal is a daily discovery of where one is on his or her journey. It has been important to me to write daily so that I might know where I am. Sometimes, the way is dark, lonely and frightening; sometimes it is lovely, fulfilling and meaningful; sometimes it is a little of both. I do not know where my journey takes me but it has been my experience that whenever I have asked I have received support from Jesus or from some other positive figure.

My journal is a place where I can consider important questions and concerns. It is a place where I can pour forth my true feelings to God. I have discovered that above all God asks me to be myself and accepts me for so being. I have found my journal to be a holy place where I can meet God. During difficult times, I have received comfort just holding my journal in my hands, for it has come to represent to me my ongoing deepening pact with God.

My journal is a friend. Through it I have made discoveries which have enriched me and have enriched my relationships with others. It is important to see the journal in context, however, for the journal is one part of a larger life. Just as my journal has affected my life so too have life experiences confirmed and enhanced my inner discoveries and pointed to new areas for exploration and consideration. My journal "works" best when it is part of my whole life, when it is "in synch" with my outer relationships, work and spiritual life. Sometimes I have used it to escape these outer facts or painful inner realities and have been rewarded in kind. But the fact of using it for an escape is then recorded and even in those times I can more adequately work through my fears and problems.

Keeping a journal has helped me become more conscious of who I am and of God's relationship with me. I have found that when I ignore it for a day or two that I begin to feel sick. I understand this to mean that by not writing I am cutting myself off from one of my primary connections with God and with myself. My journal is a record and an ongoing part of my journey.

A journal as written prayer

A priest friend who has been keeping a journal for 12 years wrote to me telling me how much his journal had meant to him. He started keeping the journal before he knew all of its possibilities. His story needs no further introduction.

Any systematic effort in journal keeping began for me in 1967 when I moved from teaching at the Prep Seminary at Notre Dame (Seminary closed in May 1967) and began a new and quite different career of work teaching at the high school in Chicago, in suburban Niles. The change was dramatic and traumatic for me; I don't think it was the change itself that started anything within myself, but the change focused my attention on what had been in process already for many years. It was with this change that I began systematically trying to understand the inner movements that were in process, by writing reflectively in my Journal the feelings and questions and doubts that were present, not only in my own mind and heart at the time, but in those years of post Vatican II, which I saw were in the minds and hearts of many others, especially my brother Priests and Religious. However, the "seed" for Journal keeping had been planted years before this time.

In 1946 I left the University of St. Mary's of Texas to come to Notre Dame and enter the Seminary. On my way to Yankeeland I stopped off in Anderson, Indiana, to visit a relative working in a hospital there. Since I was on my way to the seminary, this relative thought it fitting that I meet the Priest chaplain at the hospital and have a talk with him. I recall very little of this meeting. I don't recall the priest's name, or what he looked like, or much of anything we talked about. But one thing the priest said to me at that time, back in 1946, had always remained with me. Somewhere in the course of our conversation he said something to the effect that I should "not let a day go by without writing something for myself," it did not matter what I wrote . . . it could be writing something that happened that day, or something that I felt was important or just what happened to be on my mind at the time, but that I should write something each day.

I didn't think too much of this advice at the time. Getting into a new program, in all the requirements and activities of Notre Dame and the Seminary program, etc., I went about the required business of each day without any thought of ever writing anything down. Years later, after I was ordained and back teaching in the seminary I attended a class taught by Susan B. Anthony on "Prayer Supported Apostles." One of her suggestions was that we should write out our personal prayers as a method of praying as a device to help keep attention fixed on what we were about at the moment. Here I was, again, years later, being once again told of the value of writing "for myself." I recalled what the priest in Anderson had told me so many years before.

I have always had, since my earliest youth, the habit of rising early, and I kept this practice through the years. In those early days of my teaching career I was thoroughly habituated to this early rising; I would go down to the kitchen and brew a pot of coffee and sit there in the quiet early morning hours alone in my reflections. Recalling that I had been counseled to "write something each day" and to "write out my prayer reflections" I began to do this each morning. I began in those early years of writing prayerfully just jotting my thoughts and prayers down on a paper napkin. I would reflect and write for an hour and afterwards just throw away the napkin. This practice continued for a number of years until my move to Chicago and it occurred to me that it would be better to keep these reflections rather than throw them away. And that was when I began keeping a Journal.

Since that time I have "religiously" kept writing my Journal, and it has always been flavored by these two notions of: "writing something every day" and "writing out my prayers," i.e. it has always been for me a way of praying in and through the events of my story process and always done kinda like I was talking to the Lord through these events in my experience of my life's story.

A journal as a spiritual midwife

In the winter of 1977 a student came into my class on the Phenomenology of Religious Experience. I soon found that he had come into the class to try to understand his own inner turmoil. When he found that I could listen to individual stories as well as teach a class, he came to visit me in my office. He had been raised a strict Catholic, had come to Notre Dame and fallen into a deep agnosticism. Along with this went moral confusion and then guilt, anxiety, and even suicidal depression. Keeping a journal helped him to see that his experience was truly one of death and rebirth. He tells how his journal was an essential part of his rebirth:

Keeping a journal helped me to sort out and begin to understand the tumult that was going on inside me—it stabilized me as a sea anchor steadies a ship in a heavy storm. When particularly dark fears threatened to drive me to despair, I would write them down; and instead of thinking of them as my own thoughts somehow grown perverse, I pictured them as coming from one character in a drama going on within me, the great struggle between good and evil which had played such an important part in many myths. I pictured the dark voices as something like the servants of the Dark Lord of J. R. R. Tolkien's *Lord of the Rings,* whose presence always brought fear and despair into the hearts of the members of the quest. I realized that stories such as Tolkien's are not simply good "yarns"; they speak in symbolic terms about an actual, experienceable reality.

Through writing these experiences down, I quickly realized that these dark voices always spoke half-truths—that is, their dark pronouncements, condemning me for some past failure, or telling me I would never again be healthy or happy, trying to convince me that I was damned to destruction, were always based on a grain of truth which had been twisted into a horrible weapon to torture me. Written down, these dark pronouncements could be seen for what they were; the grain of truth could be examined and faced with honesty, and the negative exaggeration could be seen clearly, and sometimes even laughed at.

Later, when I had weathered the storm and began to see that this crisis was a spiritual "rebirth," I realized that even the urge towards suicide which the dark voices had assaulted me with was a similar twisted truth. In Charles Williams' remarkable novel *War in Heaven* I read the passage, "even the hunger for death was but a perversion of the death which precedes all holy birth." (Note: Page 242, Eerdmans Publishing Company edition) When the dark voices told me I had to die, they were in a sense correct—in St. Paul's letter, the "old man" had to die so that the "new man" could be born, the new man in whom the spirit of Christ lived (Romans 6:6-9). Jesus' statement that a man had to lose his life to gain it began to make sense for the first time.

The journal also proved invaluable in helping this process of rebirth along. Before I realized that such a process was occurring, a dream informed me of it. I dreamed that a man and a woman with an infant child and a donkey came down to the shore of a large lake which they had to cross. To do this the parents and the donkey had to swim immersed in the lake, holding the child safely above the water. It was difficult, but it appeared that they would make it. I wrote the dream in my journal, and this made it possible to reflect on its meaning later. I realized that the scene of the dream reminded me of a painting I had seen of the Holy Family's flight into Egypt after Christ's birth. Joseph had been warned in a dream to flee Herod, who would slaughter all the infants in Bethlehem in order to kill the newborn Savior.

The dream was telling me that Christ had already been born within me! I tried to help this process along by writing in my journal an elaboration of the dream, in which I tried to picture the thoughts, doubts and hopes of Joseph and Mary on such an arduous journey as they struggled to understand the amazing story they were involved in. I entered the drama myself, offering the tired travelers water and encouragement, and asking their blessing. In this way I hoped to assist the process going on within me. The effect of exercises like this was remarkable—my confidence grew, my anxiety lessened, and I began to believe for the first time in my life that Christ might be a reality, a living force in people's lives as he was to the apostles after his Resurrection. I continued to keep a daily record of my progress, nurturing the light that had been born within me.

A few weeks later I was to record an experience in my journal that I couldn't have imagined when I started it months before in darkness and confusion. The experience occurred during a mass I attended in a small chapel with a few friends. For the gospel reading Morton read the "good shepherd" passage from the Gospel of John. I had probably heard the words a hundred times, but suddenly they took on a meaning I had never seen before. Christ was describing his ability to protect the soul from evil, from dark forces such as the ones I had faced within me. At that moment I felt what I can only describe as a presence— as real as the dark voices had been real, but quite different. I felt like Christ had taken my heart into his hands and was holding it, and I understood the power that Dante had described as "the Love that moves the sun and other stars." In one moment I felt a deep sorrow and a great joy, as if Christ were showing me the depths he had touched in his suffering and the reality of his Resurrection, his defeat of the darkness. I knew that this power was stronger than the dark forces, that Christ is, as John says, "a light that the darkness could not comprehend."

This experience, too, went into my journal; and I could look back and see my progress, like Dante's in his *Divine Comedy,* from the depths of darkness to a glimpse of heavenly joy. Without the journal the journey would have been much more difficult; the stability it gave me and the help in comprehending the drama within me were invaluable.

Getting to work

This book on journal keeping is valueless until it spurs the reader into the practice of keeping a record of the inner life. It does little or no good to read about journal keeping unless one buys a journal, a pencil sacred to it, and gets to work.

Each of us has a unique destiny. Seldom do we find it unless we record our glimmerings of what it might be and move toward it. The divine lover is waiting to give us more than we can imagine, but we must move toward him. The journal is one way to pick one's self up and start moving.

One does not have to be a specially gifted religious person to start keeping a record of one's inner life. However, as one continues to use a journal one can learn how special and valuable one is to the divine other who has made us all and would draw us to the unsearchable riches of the kingdom. The possibilities described in former times are still open to those who will take the time and discipline to open themselves to the guiding spirit of God and to write down what they discover.

Bibliography

This bibliography is not exhaustive. Most of the books referred to have been mentioned in the text. It is provided for easy reference for the reader who wishes to pursue further a particular aspect of journaling.

Journaling in general

The best books on journaling are the following:

Association for Research and Enlightenment. *Workbook Journal*. Virginia Beach, Virginia, 1975.

Baldwin, Christina. *One to One: Self-Understanding Through Journal Writing*. New York: M. Evans, 1979.

Hughes, Milt. *Spiritual Journey Notebook*. National Student Ministries, 127 9th Ave. N., Nashville, Tenn. 37234 (a spiritual journal geared into Bible reading and spiritual growth).

Lindbergh, Anne Morrow. *Gift from the Sea*. New York: Random House, 1978.

Progoff, Ira. *At a Journal Workshop: The Basic Text and Guide for Using the Intensive Journal.* New York: Dialogue House, 1975.

Roh, Ray. *Keeping a Spiritual Journal.* Pecos, N.M.: Dove, 1978.

Simons, George F. *Journal for Life: Discovering Faith and Values Through Journal Keeping: Part One—Foundations.* Chicago: Life in Christ, 1975.

Simons, George F. *Journal for Life: Discovering Faith and Values Through Journal Keeping: Part Two—Theology from Experience.* Chicago: Life in Christ, 1977.

Simons, George F. *Keeping Your Personal Journal.* New York: Paulist Press, 1978.

Journals and spiritual growth

In two of my books I have discussed the value of keeping a journal as part of a growing religious life:

Kelsey, Morton T. *Encounter with God: A Theology of Christian Experience.* Minneapolis: Bethany Fellowship, 1972.

Kelsey, Morton T. *The Other Side of Silence: A Guide to Christian Meditation.* New York: Paulist Press, 1976.

In two other books I have given examples of entering imaginatively into biblical stories and into the lives of men and women of our time:

Kelsey, Morton T. *The Hinge.* King of Prussia, Penn.: Religious Publishing Co., 1977.

Kelsey, Morton T. *The Age of Miracles.* Notre Dame: Ave Maria Press, 1979.

Keeping a journal was a very important discipline in both Jung's personal life and in his therapeutic practice. Laurens van der Post has indicated the importance of Jung's journal for him in his excellent film on the life of Jung, which may be obtained from the C. G. Jung Foundation for Analytical Psychology, Inc., New York, N.Y. Jung, however, wrote little specifically on the subject. If one would get at the essential message of Jung for modern men and women I would suggest reading the following books by him in the order given:

Memories, Dreams, Reflections. New York: Random House, 1965.

Man and His Symbols. New York: Dell, 1968.

The Tavistock Lectures on the Theory and Practice of Analytical Psychology. *Collected Works,* vol. 18. Princeton: Princeton Univ. Press, 1976.

Modern Man in Search of a Soul. New York: Harcourt Brace Jovanovich, 1955.

Two Essays on Analytical Psychology. Collected Works, vol. 7. Princeton: Princeton Univ. Press, 1972.

Journals to read

Christina Baldwin notes in the bibliography to her book on journaling that there are probably some nine thousand journals and diaries in print. Everyone has their own favorites. Below are listed a few which have made a great impression on me. Some have already been mentioned in the text.

St. Augustine. *Confessions*. New York: Penguin, 1961. See also David B. Burrell's excellent commentary on the *Confessions* of Augustine in *Exercises in Religious Understanding*. Notre Dame: Univ. of Notre Dame Press, 1975.

Hammarskjöld, Dag. *Markings*. 9th ed. Salem, N.H.: Merrimack Book Service, 1965. This modern classic reveals the spiritual side of the United Nations secretary general.

Jung, C. G. *The Answer to Job*. Princeton: Princeton Univ. Press, 1972. This work, written after Jung's near-death experience, is a magnificent example of active imagination.

Merton, Thomas. *Conjectures of a Guilty Bystander*. Garden City: Doubleday, 1968.

Nijinsky, Romula, ed. *The Diary of Vaslav Nijinsky*. Berkeley: Univ. of Calif. Press, 1971. This is the tragic record of the disintegration of a great artist.

Nin, Anais. Several of her novels and diaries are marvelous examples of journaling by a friend of many literary giants.

Woolman, John. *The Journal of John Woolman*. Secancus, N.J.: Citadel Press, 1972.

Other helpful books

Bailey, Kenneth. *The Cross and the Prodigal*. St. Louis: Concordia Publishing House, 1973.

Cirlot, J. E. *A Dictionary of Symbols*. 2nd ed. New York: Philosophical Library, 1972.

Dante Alighieri. *The Divine Comedy*. New York: Random House, 1955.

Huizinga, Johan. *Homo Ludens: A Study of the Play Element in Culture*. Boston: Beacon Press, 1955.

Huxley, Aldous. *The Doors of Perception*. New York: Harper and Row, 1970.

St. John of the Cross. *Poems*. Baltimore: Penguin, 1968.

Johnston, William. *The Still Point: Reflections on Zen and Christian Mysticism*. New York: Fordham Univ. Press, 1977.

Kelsey, Morton. *Can Christians Be Educated?* Mishawaka, Ind.: Religious Education Press, 1977.

Kelsey, Morton. *Discernment, A Study in Ecstasy and Evil*. New York: Paulist Press, 1978.

Kelsey, Morton. *Dreams: A Way to Listen to God*. New York: Paulist Press, 1978.

Kelsey, Morton. *God, Dreams, and Revelation*. Minneapolis: Augsburg Publishing House, 1974.

Kelsey, Morton. *Healing and Christianity*. New York: Harper and Row, 1976.

Kelsey, Morton. *Myth, History, and Faith: The Remythologizing of Christianity*. New York: Paulist Press, 1974.

Lewis, C. S. *The Screwtape Letters*. New York: Macmillan, 1967.

Lewis, C. S. *That Hideous Strength*. New York: Macmillan, 1965.

Luke, Helen M. *Dark Wood to White Rose: A Study of Meanings in Dante's Divine Comedy*. Pecos, N.M.: Dove, 1975.

Lynch, James J. *The Broken Heart: The Medical Consequences of Loneliness*. New York: Basic Books, 1979.

Mehl, Duane. *No More for the Road: One Man's Journey from Chemical Dependency to Freedom*. Minneapolis: Augsburg Publishing House, 1976.

Phillips, Dorothy, et al., eds. *The Choice Is Always Ours: An Anthology of the Religious Way.* rev. ed. Wheaton: Theosophical Publishing House, 1975.

Rinker, Rosalind. *Prayer: Conversing with God.* Grand Rapids: Zondervan Publishing House, 1971.

Sanford, John. *Dreams and Healing: A Succinct and Lively Interpretation of Dreams.* New York: Paulist Press, 1979.

Schwenck, Robert. *Digging Deep: Penetrating Our Inner Selves Through Dream Symbols.* Pecos, N.M.: Dove, 1979.

Simonton, Carl, et al. *Getting Well Again: A Step-by-Step Self-Help Guide to Overcoming Cancer for Patients and Their Families.* New York: J. P. Tarcher, 1978.

Stewart, Mary. *The Crystal Cave.* New York: Fawcett, 1979.

Stewart, Mary. *The Hollow Hills.* New York: Fawcett, 1979.

Tillich, Paul. *The Courage to Be.* New Haven: Yale Univ. Press, 1952.

Wink, Walter. *The Bible in Human Transformation: Toward a New Paradigm for Biblical Study.* Philadelphia: Fortress Press, 1973.